What people are saying a

"Brian, you did it again, and this time you've given us a practical resource to put in the hands of every parent we partner with. For too long children's ministers have tried to do at church alone what Father God meant for parents to do. This how-to-book for parents can help arm them to do what they were created to do—raise godly kids. This is great stuff I can't wait to use myself. Children's pastors talk about the need to partner with parents, but this book shows you how!"

Jim Wideman

Author, children's pastor, and world-renowned public speaker

"The material in this book is incredibly insightful, and I'm already implementing it in my home. That's how practical and helpful it is. Brian has brought some of his best stuff to this book."

Jeremy Lee

Creator of ParentMinistry.net

"I love this book. Brian not only navigates parents through 'why' but 'how" to talk to their children about difficult topics. His simple concept of being *proactive early* rather than *reactive later* is something we all need to hear."

Craig Jutila

President of Empowered Living Inc.; author of Faith and the Modern Family: How to Raise a Healthy Family in a Modern World; *www.whowillyouempower.com*

"Discipling children is one of the most important responsibilities Christian parents have. The younger the child the more difficult it is to know what to say, how to say it, and when to say it. If you are struggling, let Brian Dollar be your coach. As you read *Talk Now and Later* you will feel as though he is by your side, coaching you every step of the way."

Dr. Alton Garrison

Assistant General Superintendent of the Assemblies of God

"What a gift! This is the easy-to-read resource church leaders have been waiting for, whether for their own reference or to provide families in their ministry. Rich with relatable stories and Bible illustrations, Brian equips parents to shepherd their children through life's toughest issues. As I read the book, I kept thinking of unchurched friends who are resistant to faith discussions but who would be receptive to this book because they want help navigating difficult parent-child discussions. This is one of the most practical and universally helpful family ministry tools I've ever seen."

Amy Fenton Lee

Author of Leading a Special Needs Ministry: A Practical Guide to Including Children and Loving Families *and blogger at* TheInclusiveChurch.com

"In easy-to-read and practical terms, Brian has taken Moses' instruction in Deuteronomy to talk about the things of God 'when you sit at home and when you walk along the road, when you lie down and when you get up' and gives clear direction to parents. This book should have a permanent spot on the nightstand of every parent whose intent is to talk with their children through life's challenges and thereby raise the next generation of strong Christians."

Dr. Greg Murry

Superintendent, Conway Public Schools

"Today's generation of children deeply desires a significant relationship with their parents. In *Talk Now and Later*, author Brian Dollar takes moms and dads to school on casual conversation with their kids. In a screen-first world, honing the skills to relate and connect to our children is critical. *Talk Now and Later* is a vital guide that provides language and biblical foundations to navigate these conversations with confidence."

Matt Guevara

Director, International Network of Children's Ministries

"Brian has a knack for infusing humor and truth with practical steps to help parents communicate with their kids. *Talk Now and Later* is appropriately named because talking with your kids now builds a relational bridge to the heart of your child that difficulty will inevitably test. Brian's insight on how to do that well is life-giving. As a pastor and parent, I see the need for this book in my life and I hope you will as well."

Sam Luce

Blogger at Samluce.com; campus pastor, Redeemer Church, Utica, NY

"Parenting in today's world is super challenging! Kids now face difficult, complex issues earlier than ever. Times have changed. Parents, don't let society, culture, and the media shape your kids' opinions. Brian Dollar provides an easy-to-read practical blueprint for difficult conversations. With his wisdom and Bible-based advice, you can lead your children through life's toughest topics. *Talk Now and Later* is a valuable guide for parents attempting to raise godly children."

Rod Loy

Senior Pastor, First Assembly of God, North Little Rock, AR; author of Three Questions, Immediate Obedience, *and* After the Honeymoon

"Years ago, I had the privilege of watching Brian from a front row seat as we served together on a church staff. I was impressed with his insights, warmth, and creativity. In the years since then, I've seen him grow into a phenomenal leader, teacher, and shepherd of kids and their parents. This book, *Talk Now and Later*, is an instant classic. As he addresses ten important topics of conversation for parents and their children, he provides clear understanding, a biblical foundation, practical suggestions, and stories that inspire and challenge parents to step into their kids' lives in a deeper way."

Scott Wilson

Senior Pastor of The Oaks Fellowship, Red Oak, TX

"Often, single parents are plagued by the task of talking to their children about topics they feel the absent parent should discuss. Brian's instruction on approaching these conversations and creating an effective dialogue with children is incredibly comforting, practical, and encouraging. Any parent in any situation can use this book. It's definitely a hands-on, must-have manual."

Renee Donaldson
Single mother of two

"There are dozens of conversations parents want to avoid having with their kids because they feel awkward, don't have the answers, or are uncertain how their kids will respond. But these conversations are critical. In *Talk Now and Later,* Brian gives practical insights to help parents introduce the topic and speak with confidence. Kids everywhere will thank their parents for reading this book . . .and putting it into practice."

Mark Entzminger
Senior Director of Children's Ministries of the General Council of the Assemblies of God

"*Talk Now and Later* is more than a discussion starter, it's a valuable tool every parent needs to raise godly children. Brian Dollar shares from his experience, education, and ministry how to navigate difficult conversations. It will encourage you, make you laugh, and, most importantly, guide you step by step so you will be equipped to point your children to

God and the Bible. You will use this book as a reference for years to come."

John Van Pay

Lead pastor, Gateway Fellowship Church, San Antonio, TX

"As a mother of five, I know firsthand how easy it is to avoid talking about tough topics with your kids. Brian tells us both why and how to have the courageous conversations necessary to raise socially, emotionally, and spiritually healthy kids. You'll find yourself reaching for this book often as you navigate your parenting journey."

Donna Hill

Mother of five and professional educator

"Kids don't come with owner's manuals. If they did, this book would be required reading. Parents will agree it's their job to have the 'uncomfortable' conversations, but too often they don't know how to start. *Talk Now and Later* provides a real life, practical resource for parents. From the introduction to the conclusion, Brian has shared principle-centered advice for parents. It's a terrific resource for anyone with children!"

Spencer Click

Executive Pastor of Family Life, Bethel Church, Hampton, VA

"To be an effective minister to kids and families, you have to connect with them and help them with the unique challenges they face. Brian has been doing this for years, and now he shares his insights with the rest of us. This book is a must-read!"

Ryan Frank

CEO and publisher, KidzMatter

Foreword by Dr. Michelle Anthony
Vice President and Publisher, Learning Resources at David C. Cook

Talk Now and Later

How to Lead Kids Through Life's Tough Topics

BRIAN DOLLAR

Published by Salubris Resources
1445 N. Boonville Ave
Springfield, Missouri 65802
www.salubrisresources.com

Cover design by Plain Joe Studios www.plainjoestudios.com
Interior formatting by Anne McLaughlin

Unless otherwise specified, Scripture quotations are taken from the Holy Bible, New Living Translation, copyright ©1996, 2004, 2007 by Tyndale House Foundation. Used by permission of Tyndale House Publishers, Inc., Carol Stream, Illinois 60188. All rights reserved.

Scripture quotations marked NKJV are from the New King James Version®. Copyright © 1982 by Thomas Nelson. Used by permission. All rights reserved.

Scripture quotations marked NIV are taken from the Holy Bible, New International Version®. , NIV®. Copyright © 1973, 1978, 1984, 2011 by Biblica, Inc. ™ Used by permission of Zondervan. All rights reserved worldwide.www.zondervan.com. The "NIV" and "New International Version" are trademarks registered in the United States Patent and Trademark Office by Biblica, Inc.™

Scripture quotations marked MSG are from *The Message*. Copyright © 1993, 1994, 1995, 1996, 2000, 2001, 2002. Used by permission of NavPress Publishing Group.

Scripture quotations marked KJV are from The King James Version of the Bible, which is in the public domain.

Note: Some names and details have been changed to protect anonymity.

ISBN: 978-1-68067-027-1

Printed in the United States of America

19 18 17 16 ● 2 3 4 5

This book is dedicated to:

My wife, Cherith.

Together, we embarked on this journey of parenthood. Although the journey is far from over, every step so far has been a blessing. Through every conversation and every tough topic, I am blessed to have a partner by my side who has such deep empathy, divine wisdom, and a heart of gold. I love you. Thanks for giving me two of the most beautiful children a man could ever hope for.

My daughter, Ashton.

You are my most beautiful angel. From the time you were born, I have seen God's hand on your life. I admire your passion for worship, and I can't wait to see what the Lord accomplishes through you. Stay close to Him, and never ever settle for anything but His best. Always remember: I love you. I'm proud of you. I'm so glad you're my daughter.

My son, Jordan.

You have been my little buddy from day one. As you enter into manhood, I eagerly anticipate what God has planned for you. Your tenacity, ingenuity, and undying love for people are going to open doors to wonderful adventures. I challenge you to remain in Him, and let His words remain in you (John 15:6). Never forget: I love you. I'm proud of you. I'm so glad you're my son.

Contents

Foreword

Think about the kind of preparation you received to be a parent *before you had children*. If you are like most, it was minimal to none. While there's quite a bit of preparation for pregnancy and the actual birth, most parents are left to figure out the rest on their own. And "the rest" is far more daunting than any of us could have ever imagined.

And if parenting isn't difficult enough, the role of the Christian parent—attempting to pass on faith to our children in a hostile world—is even *more complicated*.

As Christian parents . . . we need help. The brevity in which we have primary influence in our children's lives demands that we consider the types of things that matter most in raising kids who move past childhood beliefs into lifetime faith that endures. In fact, this book will encourage you to think deeply and creatively about your influence on your children at every age and stage throughout their entire lives.

Children living in today's world need to know their parents are willing to have the types of conversations that others in society are having with them. Parents need to be willing and equipped to have these important talks.

In this book, Brian Dollar tackles these uncharted territories with the practical ease that makes difficult conversations seem doable . . . and even desirable. Dollar teaches parents, through real-life stories and pragmatic approaches, how to build authentic relationships with their children when they are young, and then how to seamlessly navigate those relationships into the teen years with confidence and courage.

When parents read this book, they will feel encouraged and equipped, not burdened or guilt-ridden, by the biblical support and encouraging reminders that we are not parenting alone. Instead, we are parenting with God's wisdom, strength, and presence. Willing to traverse the rugged terrain of what was once considered taboo in Christian parenting, Dollar gives honest answers and insights into the difficult questions that families wrestle with every day.

Brian Dollar is no novice when it comes to these topics. In fact, he is the premiere voice to be leading this venture. With his personal stories from raising his two kids and his decades of ministry experience with children and their families, he has earned the right to lead and guide us as we parent a new generation.

This book is one that every Christian parent needs to have, read, and keep close by for the daily pressures that build up in homes that are pursuing a perfect God in less than perfect circumstances.

Dr. Michelle Anthony

Vice President and Publisher of Learning Resources at David C. Cook; Author of Spiritual Parenting, Dreaming of More for the Next Generation, The Big God Story, *and* Becoming a Spiritually Healthy Family

Introduction:

The Power of Conversation

Most of us have a dozen excuses why we don't want to talk to our kids about difficult topics. Some of the most common ones I've heard (or used myself) are:

- "I'm worried I won't say the right things."

- "I'm afraid I'll talk over her head."

- "What if he asks a question I can't answer? I don't want to look stupid!"

- "It takes too much time and effort to try to explain complex topics to a child."

- "I don't even know what I think about these topics. How in the world can I give my child good information?"

- "My kids aren't ready for this kind of conversation."

- "If I say the wrong thing, it might mess her up for the rest of her life!"

- "If I don't say anything, at least I won't say the wrong thing."

- "I'm way too busy to spend time talking about topics like this. It takes too long. And my kids are always busy, too."

- "My parents didn't talk to me about all this, and I turned out okay. Why do I need to talk to my children about it? Don't worry, they'll be fine."

Opposite Errors

Parents often make one of two opposing errors in talking to their kids. And to make things interesting, proponents of these two opposites are often married to each other! Some parents are too protective. They don't want to even mention the hard things of life to their children because they're afraid TMI (too much information—specifically, the wrong information) will give them ideas they would never have on their own. At the other extreme, some parents tell their children too much too soon. They talk to a five year old like she's an adult, sharing detailed information about relationships that don't compute in a child's brain.

Philip and Maria have two daughters, five and eight years old. Philip's parents underwent a messy, awkward, tense divorce when he was in junior high. He lived with his mother, who still hadn't fully recovered from the trauma of the divorce by the time Philip left for college. In their home, talking about his dad was strictly off limits. When his own daughters were young, Philip followed his mother's example. He tried to protect his children from any mention of strained relationships. He wanted them to have a Disneyland childhood, something that was the opposite of his painful experience.

Maria, on the other hand, grew up in a large, gregarious, open family. From her earliest memories, nothing was off limits in family discussions. They complained and they laughed, they griped and cried and hugged. For Maria, talking openly with her own girls was as natural as breathing.

Every day when Philip came home from work, his daughters ran up and hugged him. Fairly often, his standard question to them, "How was your day?" elicited long descriptions of detailed dysfunctions of family and friends. Philip often told Maria not to let the girls overhear juicy details about people in her talks with her friends, but then he realized the girls weren't *overhearing* these tidbits—Maria was talking to them *like they were her peers!* The girls loved feeling included, even when they didn't fully understand the intricate dynamics of the conflicts and tension in the relationships their mom described to them.

Philip wasn't amused.

The difference in perspectives led to loud disagreements between Philip and Maria. She insisted, "They're growing up, and they need to know how the world works. They're going to learn these things sooner or later, and I prefer that they learn from us . . . both of us!"

Philip reacted, "No! You're telling them too much—way too much. This level of information can't be good for them. They're just children. Give them time to be kids!"

Both were sure they were right, and both dug in their heels. It wasn't pretty . . . for Philip and Maria or the girls.

Normal Conversations

Many parents believe important and difficult topics shouldn't be addressed in "normal" everyday conversations. Weighty subjects, they assume, need only be discussed once. That should do it, and it probably should happen only when a crisis forces everyone to confront the problem.

Instead, the lines of communication need to be open so that important topics are discussed as part of the ebb and flow of normal interaction. That's the difference between a proactive parent and a reactive parent. When we keep the communication lines open, we train our kids that nothing is off limits. They're welcome to ask any questions as they arise, and we're free to say, "I don't know about that. I'll find out, and we'll talk again."

Reactive parents are caught off guard when something happens and their kids need to talk. Their communication isn't carefully planned before they speak, so it's often unclear and emotional—they're trying to patch the hole in the boat as it's sinking! Or at the other extreme, they insist nothing is wrong when something clearly needs attention—they ask, "What hole in the boat? I don't see a hole." Neither of these approaches gives adequate information and support to the child, and it sends a clear and destructive message that important topics make people freak out!

> We can prepare them by talking openly— and age-appropriately—so they're ready when the time comes to process these events.

In this book, we'll look at ten common topics your child is dealing with—or almost certainly *will* deal with in the coming years. One of our most important tasks as parents is to prepare them to think clearly and respond wisely. We can prepare them by talking openly—and age-appropriately—so they're ready when the time comes to process these events.

It isn't essential to personally experience all these things before imparting knowledge and wisdom. Quite often, kids learn vicariously as the family together observes how other families wrestle with difficult situations. In any community or church family, people experience all kinds of heartaches and setbacks. As we watch, we have the opportunity to have open, insightful conversations about how another family copes with tragedy.

For instance, a community near us was devastated by a tornado. Homes were destroyed, and a few lives were lost. Virtually every person in the community knew someone whose life was turned upside down by the storm. Cherith, Ashton, Jordan, and I talked about what those people must have experienced during the wild winds of the tornado, how they absorbed the truth that they had lost everything, and how they were trusting God with all of it: grieving the loss, rebuilding their lives, and experiencing God's goodness and strength in the middle of it all. One particular family captured our attention. We watched as they were overwhelmed with emotion, but then saw their faith grow even stronger through the ordeal. That family's experience taught our family so much.

We've also had rich conversations as we've seen families fall apart as they suffered through divorce, a death in the family, financial collapse, addiction, and other heartaches. Their experiences and responses taught our kids as much as seeing those who courageously took steps of faith.

Here's the point: Don't wait until something happens in your family to have these conversations. Have them early, have them often, and have them wisely. Then, when a crisis occurs, you have a track record of communication about the topic. You aren't flooding them with new information at a critical moment; you're helping them apply the information they've already gathered. During crises, powerful emotions often fog the brain—for the kids and the parents. It's far better to reinforce information that's already there than to introduce new concepts.

Many parents feel inadequate, insecure, and ill-equipped to have these conversations. They bring their kids to church and expect the children's ministry team or youth pastor and volunteers to fill in the gaps. That's not our role. Certainly, our responsibility is to shepherd the children, but it's also to equip parents to teach, train, and model God's principles to their kids.

Today, a growing number of children are raised by members of the extended family, primarily grandparents and aunts and uncles. If this is the case for you, every point addressed to parents in this book also applies to those who have assumed the parental role in the lives of children. If you are one of these people, I applaud you. You have stepped into the gap to provide love, stability, and direction for kids who desperately need you. You're reading this book because you want to give the very best care you can give to the children you love.

Look for Cues

If we take time to notice, we'll see times when our kids are open to talk. Too often we don't notice because we're preoccupied with our own stresses, our own agendas, and our own desires. Children often give us verbal and nonverbal cues that "the door is open and you're welcome to come in."

For instance, when I pick up Jordan from school, I always ask how his day went. Frequently he dives in to tell me about the important events of his day. If I'm paying attention, I may detect his perception of a teacher, a friend, or a challenge he has faced during the day. And if I notice, I can invite him to tell me more—not by asking probing questions that may seem intrusive, but by saying something like, "Tell me more about your lunch with Jim. It sounds like something happened between the two of you."

Sometimes, though, Jordan looks a bit discouraged and says only, "It was okay." That's a loud and clear message that his day certainly wasn't okay! At that point I have several options. I might ignore his comment and assume he'll process any problems on his own; I might try to encourage him with a fatherly pep talk ("Hey, cheer up. Life is hard, but you'll make it!"); or I can open the door myself and say simply, "Looks like you've had a hard day." No condemnation, no advice, and no smothering with affirmations . . . just an invitation to tell me as much as he wants to share.

He may respond with a short, cryptic answer like, "Bobby was a jerk, that's all."

Again, I have the same range of options. I can say, "Yes, son, people can be jerks, but you just have to toughen up"; I can ignore his comment and talk about something else; or I can say, "Tell me more about that."

Many times our kids want to talk about things that haven't crossed our minds. We may have an agenda for a conversation, but they're on a different planet. Parents need to be able to read their kids' body language and tone of voice. When one of them brings up a topic, it's important to zero in on that issue and draw the child out. But then, some kids have a hundred random topics in a day. If we have something more important to discuss, we can tell them we'll get back to theirs later and address the topic we planned to discuss.

> **Many times our kids want to talk about things that haven't crossed our minds.**

To be honest, Cherith is a hundred times better at picking up on our kids' cues than I am. She's a master at asking "one more question" to peel back another layer of emotions and perceptions to connect with our kids at a deeper level, yet even my lesser skills pay big dividends with Ashton and Jordan.

I'm convinced kids communicate all kinds of things in unguarded moments that many of us miss. If we see the cues, we then have several options: to correct, to smother, to ignore, or to engage. I suggest we engage! The goal in these conversations is to provide understanding and support, not to instantly fix the problem or avoid a difficult issue.

A Sliding Scale

Psychologists identify distinct stages of development from infancy, through childhood, to adulthood. As parents, we need to understand how much to explain at each level of development. Childhood sees the most changes in cognitive, emotional, and relational development in the shortest period of time. Each child is different; some are more advanced than others, but it's helpful to get a good grasp of these stages so we don't talk over their heads or insult them with baby talk.

Think about luggage. You don't ask a six year old to carry a one-hundred-pound suitcase. In fact, you don't give him a forty-pound suitcase. You give him a backpack or a little rolling case that weighs about seven pounds. As he grows older and stronger, he can handle a bigger load at each stage of physical development. It's the same for your children's emotional, relational, and spiritual development: give them as much as they can handle, but no more.

We can look at several identifiable stages in the growth of children:

Preschoolers

Young children are very concrete. They can't grasp abstract principles and processes. A dad came to me with a perplexed look on his face. He said, "I need some help. How can I explain the virgin birth to my little girl? She's four years old."

I answered, "I'm not sure why you need to explain that concept to your daughter. If you want to tell her anything about it, just tell her that God formed Jesus in His mother's tummy. That's all she needs to know. I think any attempt to explain the hypostatic union is a bit too much!"

Most preschoolers accept this simple answer. If, though, one of them asks, "What makes this special about Jesus? How is He different from everybody else?" a parent can explain, "The amazing thing is that Jesus was in heaven, but He decided to come to earth to be with us. To do that, He had to be born, and Mary was His mother. God became a human baby."

Elementary to middle school

Children in grade school are learning to process more information, but they still don't have the ability to analyze complex concepts. As they progress through these grades, parents should gradually give them more analysis and explanation. If they don't understand, try again and be a bit more concrete; however, you may find that they are far more intellectually advanced than you imagined.

Invite them to ask anything at all. Use their questions as a guide to the depth of the information you give them. Value all the questions they ask, but remember to frame the answer with age-appropriate, concrete, specific terms and concepts.

Age twelve and up

Beginning in the last year of middle school, everything is on the table. Our children are hearing all kinds of information from their peers—true and false, helpful and destructive—so don't be shy about wading in to talk about any subject. Some parents assume their kids are protected from certain topics because they're in a "good Christian school." Don't believe it. In any school, kids are talking about every conceivable topic from every possible angle.

When I say "everything is on the table," I mean that every topic is fair game and all questions should be honored, but it doesn't mean gossip or slander is acceptable. The guidelines for talking with older children are the same as for conversations with adults. We speak the truth, but always with wisdom and love.

When connections are based on mutual respect, each person's story is valued—even the parents'! You may think your kids don't care what happened to you when you were young. After all, isn't that when saber-toothed tigers still roamed America? But most teenagers are very interested in the struggles and triumphs of their parents and grandparents. Of course, be sensitive and discreet, but be honest about your hopes and fears, your failures and successes. Some teenagers will want to know far more than you want to tell them, and others will look incredibly bored with the first words from your mouth. Don't reveal too much, and don't push it, but use your story as a starting point for illustrations in your conversations with them about relevant topics.

As kids grow, they'll become more aware of the world around them. They may not sit down and watch the news with you or read the paper, but they may say, "What's this I hear about tornados killing a lot of people . . . or Muslims cutting off people's heads . . . or an election?" Teenagers may seem disinterested in the news, but often that's only because they don't want to appear interested in the things that interest us!

Diane Levin, Professor of Education at Wheelock College, gives this advice to parents about connecting with their kids around the news:

> The most important thing is to have open, honest, and age-appropriate conversations; and to make them part of everyday life. Creating an ongoing relationship with your child around issues in the news makes it normal for your kids to discuss upsetting or confusing events. When you do this, they see you as someone to help sort things out. You are also exposing them to the real world and helping them grow up to be informed, knowledgeable citizens who keep up with the news.[1]

Principles of Communication

Before we dive into the ten crucial topics that every family needs to address at one time or another, let's identify and describe some principles that guide our attitudes and our words.

Connections take time.

Many parents feel uncomfortable with certain topics, and they conclude that one conversation is enough. It never is. If a subject is so threatening that it makes us uncomfortable to talk about it, we need to talk about it more, not less. The ten topics in this book are some of the most important ones I've seen in the lives of families. Wise parents bring these things up before there's a crisis. When a calamity occurs, emotions run high and threats multiply. It's far better to have a long track record of good discussions, with open interaction and mutual respect, before any crisis happens.

> **If a subject is so threatening that it makes us uncomfortable to talk about it, we need to talk about it more, not less.**

All of us are learning.

I've watched as parents assumed the role of "the experts" in talking to their children about important matters. When kids are little, the parent's role of teacher is unavoidable, but as they grow up, we need to communicate increasingly that we're all in the process of learning and growing. When teenagers sense their parents are still open to new perspectives and ideas, they'll be far more willing to enter into meaningful dialogue.

Don't talk down to them.

Similarly, one of the most important principles about talking with kids is to avoid being condescending. Some parents have told me they want to "dumb down" communication with their kids. If they mean they're trying to talk on the child's level, that's a good strategy. My guess, though, is that the term *dumb down* implies two incorrect and destructive assumptions: that the child is inferior, and the parent is superior. Kids pick up on this perspective, and they deeply resent it.

We need to avoid the attitude: "I'm going to tell you what you need to know so you can become like me." No one likes paternalism—especially teenagers who are beginning to value independence and carve out their own identities! Instead, we should communicate with our words and attitudes, "These are complex topics. A lot of people have wrestled with these issues, and our family needs to wrestle with them, too. I value your ideas."

Of course, this means that we don't rush through an answer when a little child asks a question, and we don't react with disgust when teenagers voice views that are very different from our own. We don't have to agree, but we need to listen and ask follow-up questions instead of shutting the youngster down. "I don't know if I agree, but tell me more of what you're thinking" shows far more respect than, "I can't believe that's what you think!"

Don't lecture, don't laugh, don't dismiss the kid's input, and don't talk to your child like he's dumb or a fool. I list these errors because I've seen them so many times (and truthfully, I've made them far too often myself).

I often tell parents to think of themselves as missionaries to a foreign culture. When missionaries travel to the other side of the world or the other side of town, they put the gospel in the language of the people they're trying to reach, but that's not all. They also work hard to understand the foreign culture so they can put their messages into an appropriate context. Parents will greatly enhance communication with their kids if they do the same thing: adapt every message to the language and context of their kids' worlds. It takes some work to understand the younger culture, but it's well worth the effort.

Learn to ask great questions and to listen more than you talk.

Children certainly need adequate information, but they also need to feel valued and respected. Parents should ask a lot of questions rather than simply dispensing information "you need to know."

One of the most important communication tools for anyone in any relationship is the ability to ask great questions. All questions are not equal! A parent may ask, "Why in the world did you do that? What were you thinking?" but questions like these don't stimulate meaningful interaction! They are rhetorical questions that are actually statements: "You're so dumb. You obviously weren't thinking at all!"

Some questions are conversation stoppers, but others are fertilizer for rich interaction. Good questions, spoken with respect and openness, open dialogue with your children so they can tell you what they perceive about a particular event, person, or topic. We might ask:

"Why do you think that happened?"

"What are some positive things that might result from that choice?"

"What might be some unforeseen consequences of that decision?"

"How do you think God feels about that?"

And as we've already mentioned, the best statement to draw out a person isn't a question at all. It's simply, "Tell me more about that."

Other questions can start good conversations:

"What's the best thing that happened to you today?"

"Who made you laugh?"

"What's one thing you learned today?"

"When were you totally bored?"

"Who did you see being kind to someone today?"

There are no dumb questions.

It's the nature of little children to be creative and spontaneous, and it's the nature of teenagers to test their parents. In both cases, kids may ask off-the-wall questions—either because they simply don't understand the issues, or to push back to see if the parents really respect them. For any age group of children, parents need to realize there are no dumb questions.

In a talk about a family member's death, a young child may ask, "Will our dog Muffy go to heaven?" A distraught parent may initially be deeply grieved or offended by this comment. But even during times of emotional turmoil, parents should keep in mind the child's world and context.

When a child asks a question that may seem inappropriate, ask yourself, "What does this question mean to my son or daughter?" Enter the child's world and give an appropriate, loving answer. If you dismiss the question for any reason, you're communicating, "Your thoughts and feelings are bizarre and irrelevant." This message is deeply hurtful and corrosive to the relationship. The child will think twice about asking again.

Every question should be treated with the same weight of importance and value.

Every question should be treated with the same weight of importance and value. It may be harder to treat innocuous or defiant questions with respect, but those need it even more.

If the child won't talk, be gracious and patient, but don't give up.

A child may "go dark" for any number of reasons. An event, such as a death, may have traumatized the child;

the child may normally withdraw under pressure and process things internally before speaking; or there may not be enough trust for the child to speak up. In these cases don't press too hard, but don't withdraw too far. Often, nonverbal communication is the gateway to the heart. Give a hug, go for a drive to a favorite spot, or just spend time together some other way without talking about the topic.

When the time is right—and every parent has to figure out when that is, either by instinct or trial and error—gently ask an open-ended question and wait for an answer. The Lord gave us two ears and one mouth, so it's a good guideline in every relationship to listen twice as much as we talk. That's especially true when we're trying to connect with a quiet child.

If the child begins to talk, again, don't press too hard too soon. The first goal is to build trust, not to force-feed information or demand communication at a deeper level. Be gracious and kind. Acknowledge the little response you get, and then say, "Thanks. Maybe we can talk more about this sometime." And then look for another opening at a later time.

All kids are different, even (or especially) siblings. If I try to press my daughter Ashton to talk to me, she withdraws, and it takes a lot longer for her to feel comfortable than if I'm more tactful and patient at the beginning. I've learned to notice when she's reluctant to talk, so I may say, "When you're ready to talk about this, let me know. I may ask you about it later to see if you're ready."

It's perfectly natural for any of us to feel uncomfortable talking about something when we feel disturbed. Before long, though, an atmosphere of love and understanding invites us to begin a conversation. However, if a child (or adult) never wants to talk, especially after a traumatic event, that's a sign of a deeper wound that needs to be healed. A parent's evident frustration may only drive the child deeper into silence. Kindness over time can make a world of difference. When even this doesn't work to draw the child out, the child may need professional help to reveal and address the deep wounds and feelings of hopelessness and isolation.

In some families, the unwritten but clear rules have been, "Don't talk, don't feel, and don't trust." When a crisis occurs, the members of these families don't immediately start talking openly and freely, sharing their deepest feeling, and trusting each other by being vulnerable! In a crisis, they talk, feel, and trust even less. Oh, they may talk, but it's often blaming and attacking, not searching for understanding and communicating support.

A crisis often reveals the condition of an individual's heart and the hidden dynamics of a family. When the worst happens and family communications turn either ice cold or lava hot, all isn't lost. This is a wakeup call for the parents to begin working hard to change the environment of the family. It's never too late. It takes time, effort, courage, and wisdom to help kids unlearn a harmful coping strategy and adopt a new, healthy one, but it's worth it. It's well worth it.

Be willing to apologize.

Parents mess up. All parents mess up. Even deeply committed Christian parents mess up. But not all parents are willing to admit it. Some of the most wonderful words children of all ages can hear from parents are, "I was wrong. I'm so sorry. Please forgive me. I won't do it again." Apologies are necessary for individual offenses, but parents also need to address prolonged, harmful patterns of communication—demanding too much, blaming, withdrawing, smothering, and so on.

The offending parent needs to own the offenses, apologize, repent, and begin to rebuild trust.

In many cases, parents can and should explain how their painful backgrounds have colored their perceptions and shaped their responses. These stories help the rest of the family understand how they got this way, but they aren't excuses for bad behavior. The offending parent needs to own the offenses, apologize, repent, and begin to rebuild trust. A full apology communicates, "I get it now. I realize how I've hurt you, and I'm deeply sorry. I want to open the lines of communication with you. I'll do my very best to do better, and I need your help. Will you tell me when I mess up again? I have a long way to go, but I'm stepping onto the road today."

This isn't just a theory. I've had these conversations with my kids. I have asked Ashton and Jordan to speak up anytime I become condescending or demanding, and I've promised that I'll respect them when they have the courage to call me on my personal shortcomings. That means I don't get angry when they're honest with me. I don't walk off in a huff, and I don't look for some reason to blame them and turn the conversation around. I take it like a man and thank them for their courage and love.

For instance, I get upset when mechanical things don't work. I won't go into the deep, psychological reasons for my sense of electronic entitlement, but you can be sure that if a computer program or a television remote or a lamp doesn't work the way I want it to work, my reaction isn't pretty! When my face gets red, I begin to growl, and it looks like I'm going to yank the cord out of the wall, Ashton and Jordan can say, "Patience, Dad." That's enough to remind me of my commitment to them to maintain my cool.

When they speak up, I don't bark, "You can't tell me to be patient! Can't you see that this darn thing isn't working?" Instead, I thank them for their loving reminder. My relationship with them is far more important than my desire to have electronic components run smoothly. And because I have asked for their input, they are validated as valued, respected people.

Watch the body language—yours and theirs.

Research indicates that body language accounts for 50 to 70 percent of communication.[2] We may not be completely aware of the impact of facial expressions, eye contact, and other nonverbal cues, but they powerfully shape the messages we send and receive. Our body language—a smile or frown, crossed or relaxed arms, etc.—may reinforce what we're saying, or it may completely contradict our words. I've watched parents with stern expressions growl to a little child, "You know I love you, don't you?" Well, no, the child doesn't know the parent loves her if the expression doesn't match the words!

Eye contact and facial expression can send a clear message. We don't really need words to let someone know, "I'm completely absorbed in what you're saying," or, "You're in big trouble!" And when people don't maintain eye contact, it almost certainly is a sign of insecurity. The issue is not necessarily that the speaker is offensive and demanding. Perhaps other factors have caused the listener to feel insecure, such as guilt, failure, or unsettling events that have nothing to do with the current conversation.

Parents, be good students of your body language, and make the necessary adjustments to ensure your verbal and nonverbal messages are consistent . . . and positive. Also be a good student of your children's body language. It often tells you more than their words can ever say.

Now that I've said body language is really important, I'll hedge a little. Some of the best conversations I have with my kids, and especially Jordan, are in the car when both of us are facing forward. Neither of us has to worry about eye contact, facial expressions, or anything like that. For some reason, this seating arrangement frees us up to have some of our most meaningful talks.

With Ashton, the dynamic is completely different. Our best talks are when just the two of us are in a room and we're completely absorbed in each other. We sit face to face, and we both notice all the cues in the room. (Well, at least she does. I probably notice about 20 percent of them!) To Ashton, the nonverbals make the conversation.

Prepare your response.

Older kids sometimes (maybe often) test their parents by saying things meant to be shocking. When this happens, don't take the bait. Act like you're playing poker in the saloon in an old western. Keep a straight face, nod that you heard the comment, and say something like, "Interesting. What do you think about it?"

When children begin to challenge their parents, the parents need to do some evaluation and planning before responding. They can ask themselves, "How are we going to respond—or react—when Jim or Janie tell us something designed to elicit outrage or shock?" I suggest they role-play and practice their responses. They can look in the mirror to see the expression on their faces when a spouse plays the role of the child and says something like, "By the way, I'm pregnant," "Johnny set himself on fire," or "Mom and Dad, how do you like the dragon tattoo . . . on my neck?"

In tense moments in relationships, people often make one of two mistakes: they "get big" or they "get little." They get big by talking loudly, leaning forward, glaring, and making demands. Or they get little by slumping in the chair, looking down, mumbling inaudibly, and giving in to any perceived threat. This response doesn't happen just once; it becomes the pattern of every significant and difficult interaction. Both responses are attempts to gain control—one by making demands and not taking no for an answer, and the other by giving in to resolve the conflict as soon as possible. And they work! The "big" person "wins" the argument, and the "little" person gets it over quickly. So everybody feels better, but only for a moment. The damage is ongoing because these misguided coping strategies significantly erode trust and create deeper divisions.

In a family, the dynamics among all the "big" people and "little" people get very interesting. If a sensitive child sees one parent continually give in to avoid conflict or end it quickly, she may adopt the same maneuver. And if another child sees the other parent win by getting big, he may emulate that behavior. Rather than working toward a mutual goal of building trust and speaking the truth in love, each person's goal is merely to win the latest round of dominance and compliance. But this game has no winners. It only creates all kinds of interesting power plays.

If parents are aware of their normal responses to difficult conversations, they'll be able to make choices before, during, and after their conversations with their kids. It's hard to change the pattern of a lifetime, but for some parents, it's necessary if they want to create an environment where people feel valued and vulnerable without risk.

Know your child.

Children are anything but static creatures. They're enormously complex, and they change from one stage to the next. Gender, personality, experiences, and age all play vital roles in how they process the ups and downs of life. And each child, even within a family, can be very, very different. Our task as parents is to notice what makes each of our children tick and then tailor our communication to fit that child in that situation.

> **Our task as parents is to notice what makes each of our children tick and then tailor our communication to fit that child in that situation.**

To complicate matters, the parents may have had very different experiences when they were children. A mom who was tenderly nurtured as a child may want her teenage son to keep snuggling with her, but it's not going to happen! She can get frustrated and assume there's something wrong with the relationship, or she can realize he's becoming a man and needs plenty of independence—and independence isn't rejection.

Many parents do well with their kids when they're small, but they don't understand what's going on in adolescence. Teenagers (and perhaps young people into their twenties) are developing their sense of identity—an identity that's separate from their parents. This doesn't mean they'll run away and never come back, but the normal, healthy process of becoming an adult requires them to increasingly become self-reliant instead of remaining dependent on their parents. In *North and South*, novelist Elizabeth Gaskell has Mr. Hale giving this advice to Margaret about raising adolescents:

> "Now, the error which many parents commit in the treatment of the individual at this time is, insisting on the same unreasoning obedience as when all he had to do in the way of duty was, to obey the simple laws of 'Come when you're called' and 'Do as you're bid!' But a wise parent humors the desire for independent action, so as to become the friend and adviser when his absolute rule shall cease."[3]

When teenagers push back, understand that's part of the program for them to grow up and become adults. They're trying out their independence on you. Instead of feeling threatened and putting the clamps down on them, learn to work with them to give them a powerful combination of roots and wings—roots of security and wings to fly and try new things. They're going to get some things wrong. That's guaranteed. But a parent's overreaction to their attempts at independence produces defiance, not trust.

Of course, I'm not saying that parents should affirm everything a teenager does. That would be malpractice on my part and foolish for the parents. There are times when we have to set limits and impose consequences, but those limits shouldn't be too confined or too harsh.

Gradually, as the children grow up, take on more responsibilities, learn from their failures, and craft their own identities, we can have an adult-adult relationship with them. For some, that happens early, but other kids tend to remain emotionally (and maybe financially) dependent for the rest of their lives. Don't let that happen! Let their roots sink deep into your love and acceptance, and give them strong wings to fly on their own. They'll be tremendously grateful, and you'll have a wonderful connection for the rest of your lives.

We shouldn't expect two parents to completely agree on every aspect of parenting, but a couple needs to work hard to find enough agreement to present a united front to the children.

Same-Page Parenting

We shouldn't expect two parents to completely agree on every aspect of parenting, but a couple needs to work hard to find enough agreement to present a united front to the children. Almost invariably, one is stricter than the other, one is more affectionate than the other, and one is more generous with time and money than the other. These aren't huge problems . . . unless they remain unresolved.

When parents aren't on the same page, the child gets mixed signals, which is terribly confusing. She isn't sure who is right and who is wrong, who carries the weight in the family and who is weak. The child instinctively wonders, "Why are you both telling me what to do when you haven't even talked to each other? You're trying to convince me, but you haven't convinced each other."

This sets up a destructive triangle: the child naturally sides with the lenient parent against the stronger, stricter one. But if the two begin to talk behind the other parent's back, they form an alliance that is complete with espionage, secrets, and sneak attacks. In this war, nobody wins.

I recommend that parents "have the conversation before the conversation." In other words, before talking to their child about anything important, from cleaning his room to a death in the family, they need to talk with each other to resolve differences and find common ground. This isn't optional; it's mandatory for the health of the marriage and the emotional health of the child.

It's a given that two parents won't agree on everything. They don't have to, but they need to agree on how they present a point to their kids. Cherith and I disagree on many particulars about life and parenting, but that's not a problem. Over the years, we've had many conversations about how to present things to our kids. Many times, we saw things differently. We looked at facts, people, and priorities in different ways, but we always (or almost always) talked long enough and well enough so that we agreed on the approach to take with our kids. Often, we decide to focus on the 85 percent we agree on, not the 15 percent where we have differences.

Another point of contention can be the communication style. Let me tell you about the different backgrounds of a couple named David and Faith. Faith grew up in a loud family. When they were happy, they yelled; when they were angry, they yelled; when they were sad, they yelled. Faith internalized this style of communication. Her family environment shaped her expectations of how a family operates. On the other hand, David's parents were extremely quiet. In addition, their work schedules left him on his own almost every day after school. David's house was more like a morgue; Faith's was like a football stadium at the last play of a tied game! With these two divergent backgrounds, Faith and David have had to talk a lot about what good communication looks like—between them and with their kids.

If parents are divorced, it's even more important for them to get on the same page in parenting their child. Far too often, unresolved resentment poisons the communication about the other parent. Don't let this happen! Don't ask your child to take sides. You may want a confidant who understands and supports your cause against the spouse who hurt you, but don't use your child as your therapist. Find someone else. Work especially hard to communicate thoroughly, positively, and frequently with the other parent, and whenever you can, find agreement about the issues related to your child. If at all possible, don't pick fights. Find positive things about the other parent's point of view, and reinforce those. (The issue of divorce is further addressed in Chapter 6.)

If parents learn to value each other's perspectives, they can both add to the child's development instead of going to battle each day. And family discussions can be much richer. When the swords are sheathed, even the conflicts between husband and wife can be wonderful examples to the child about how to disagree agreeably. I'm not advocating conformity, but *unity out of diversity*. As Ashton and Jordan have grown, Cherith and I sometimes talk to them about our differences on an issue. If we discuss them openly, with respect instead of demands for compliance, our kids learn that having differing opinions doesn't wreck a relationship. This, I'm sure, will serve them well in every important relationship for the rest of their lives.

The Real Goal

As parents our goal isn't to rush in and have one "fix it" conversation when a crisis arises. Our goal is to create a warm, open environment where these topics are part of the fabric of family communication. We're not trying to "solve a problem"; we're trying to open channels so that every person in the family feels valued, understood, and inspired.

The qualities of communication we pour into our children will have a lasting legacy. No matter how painful or difficult our childhood might have been, we have the privilege and responsibility to create something new and wonderful for our kids—and through them, their kids and grandkids.

> **No matter how painful or difficult our childhood might have been, we have the privilege and responsibility to create something new and wonderful for our kids**

When we talk to our children about important issues, we shouldn't get upset if they don't seem to pay attention or if they resist our point of view. If our measuring stick is immediate change or agreement, we'll feel frustrated most of the time.

Each conversation is an investment in the life of your children. Have a lot of them, and they'll pay handsome dividends down the road. Like many investments, it takes a long time to see the account build and the return to be noticeable, but sooner or later, the payoff will come. I can't tell you how many parents have told me that years later, their kids remembered talks—and specific points in those talks—when the parents thought they hadn't even been listening. Kids listen far more than we realize.

Every conversation is a spiritual conversation. This doesn't mean we use "God talk" in every sentence and quote Scripture every time we talk to our kids. But it means the Word of God informs every decision we make and the Spirit of God guides us each step of the way. Parents don't have to be Bible scholars, but they can read and study enough to let the truth of God sink deep into their attitudes and actions. When our children know we're trusting God for wisdom and direction, they sense a need to trust Him, too. Our hunger for God and His Word is contagious. Our kids may look bored sometimes, and they may not like what the Bible says, but that's part of learning, growing, and internalizing the truths of Scripture and the grace of God in our lives.

Many parents feel exasperated when they think of talking to their kids about important or uncomfortable things. Whether they feel unsure or confident, the Father stands ready to hear their prayers for wisdom and clarity. We can pray before we talk to our children and trust Him to guide our thoughts and plans for the conversation, and we can pray at the end of the conversation—preferably, with the kids—to entrust everything to Him and ask for understanding, love, and strength for the future. In most of these talks, the kids aren't bored in the least. They're "dialed in" and want to know what their parents are thinking and feeling. They may not agree, and they may be confused about some issues, but unresolved points in the discussion leave the door open to further interactions.

In your prayer and in the conversation, let your children know you want to honor the Lord, you want God to give your family an abundance of love for each other, and you want to have a positive influence on other kids and their families.

You Can Do It!

You don't have to be a social worker or a psychologist to understand these issues enough to have meaningful conversations with your kids. You don't have to be a pastor or know how to pray eloquently to lead your family in prayer about a tender topic. It means everything to your kids when you take the initiative to stop and talk to God in a normal voice with an open heart. And you don't need to pray for twenty minutes. Just tell God that you need His help, you're looking to Him for direction, and you're grateful for the conversation. That's enough. If you haven't prayed with your children before, it may feel awkward at first. Push through that feeling. You'll get more comfortable as you have more experience. It's important. Let your kids know you want and need God to be in the center of your family's life.

In fact, you're probably not an expert on any of the topics covered in this book. Admit to your kids that you're learning, too—and actually be a learner. Read, ask questions, and find out more than you knew before. At every point, take the initiative to begin these conversations and share what you know. Your kids will undoubtedly ask questions or voice opinions that challenge you. Don't let that throw you. Instead of reacting, say something like, "Let me find out more about that, and you can find out more too. Then let's talk again about it and see where we go. We're going to trust God to give us wisdom about this."

Any of us can take the initiative to begin the conversation, admit we don't have all the answers, and explain that we're trusting God for direction. If we do those three things, we've taken enormous strides in being the parents God wants us to be for our children. This attitude and these actions break down walls between our kids and us. We become a little more vulnerable, which gives them permission to be a little more honest and open. As conversations progress and become a normal part of your relationship with your kids, they'll realize you aren't out to control them; you respect them, and you want God's best for them.

Each of the topics in this book contains information for you, biblical principles, stories and illustrations, and suggestions for discussions. Parents can use this book in several different ways. You can read through the book to get an idea of what's there so you'll be ready when an event needs to be addressed. You might wait until an issue surfaces in the life of the family or in a child's life, and then read the appropriate chapter and open a dialogue with the child. Or you can use the topics and questions to generate rich conversations in an ongoing series of discussions with your kids. If you talk about these important issues before a crisis occurs, everyone in the family will have a head start in responding with grace and truth.

However you choose to use this book, realize that many dynamics are at play in a family. Take the initiative, but don't push too hard. Be a learner, and value the process for everyone involved as they wrestle with these difficult topics.

In one of his letters to the Christians in Thessalonica, Paul gave advice we can apply to our relationships with our kids:

> Live peacefully with each other. . . . We urge you to warn those who are lazy. Encourage those who are timid. Take tender care of those who are weak. Be patient with everyone. (1 Thess. 5:13–14)

chapter 1

How to Talk to Your Kids About God

In my twenty-two years as a kids' pastor, I can't tell you how many times a parent has walked up to me after church and said, "My son was asking me questions about baptism last night. Would you meet with him to explain what water baptism is all about?" I've received countless emails that say something like, "My daughter asked me what it means to be saved. I don't want to confuse her, so can I set her up an appointment with you this week? I'm sure you can explain it better than I can." Parents have asked me to talk to their kids about every conceivable spiritual question. I'm happy to help, but the primary resources for these kids should be their own parents.

Too often, parents and grandparents believe they aren't qualified to impart spiritual wisdom to kids. Many parents are hesitant to take on the role of primary spiritual influence in their kids' lives for several reasons:

- They're concerned they won't say the right words or they won't be able to communicate in a way the child understands.

- They're worried their child will ask them a question they don't know the answer to—and then they'll look stupid.

- They believe theological concepts are just too hard to understand—for themselves as well as their kids—and aren't willing to put in the time and effort it takes to shape their son's or daughter's spiritual life.

- They don't want to fail at something so important, so they don't even try.

I understand the hesitation. You love your kids. You want them to grow in their relationship with God, and you don't want to "mess that up." You don't feel equipped to speak about deep spiritual issues on a child's level. That's the normal response of most parents, but it's completely off base.

Let me take you off the hook . . . at least a little bit. It's not entirely your fault you feel this way. In fact, I have a confession to make: I, along with the church as a whole for the last few decades, have gotten in the way of parents being the first and primary spiritual resource for their kids. In many ways, we (church leaders in general and children's ministers specifically) are to blame. We have hijacked the spiritual development of kids by promoting the idea that a "professional children's minister" is the only qualified, competent person to speak spiritual truth into children's lives. To some degree, we've developed a "savior complex," elevating our roles as the highest and best source of spiritual input for kids. Though we didn't plan it, this perspective lowered parents to second-class status. Ultimately, we became a hindrance to God's plan. Here's the truth: God's plan is for *parents* to be the primary spiritual leaders of their children.

> **God's plan is for *parents* to be the primary spiritual leaders of their children.**

It's Your Privilege . . . and Responsibility

God instituted the family long before He created the church, and kids' ministry leaders came along many centuries later. The first chapters of Genesis establish the family as the primary social unit under the leadership of God. When the people of God left Egypt and were on their way to the Promised Land, Moses had plenty of time to teach them about God's plans for every area of their lives, including their families. In the desert, Moses clearly outlined the ministry of the priests, yet he also explained the parents' role:

> But watch out! Be careful never to forget what you yourself have seen. Do not let these memories escape from your mind as long as you live! And be sure to pass them on to your children and grandchildren. Never forget the day when you stood before the Lord your God at Mount Sinai, where he told me, "Summon the people before me, and I will personally instruct them. Then they will learn to fear me as long as they live, and they will teach their children to fear me also." (Deut. 4:9–10)

But Moses wasn't finished. Spiritual input wasn't to be reserved for one day a week. Parents were to live and love and model biblical truth all day every day:

> So commit yourselves wholeheartedly to these words of mine. Tie them to your hands and wear them on your forehead as reminders. Teach them to your children. Talk about them when you are at home and when you are on the road, when you are going to bed and when you are getting up. Write them on the doorposts of your house and on your gates. (Deut. 11:18–20)

Solomon and Paul continued to explain the central role of parents in the spiritual nurture of children:

Direct your children onto the right path, and when they are older, they will not leave it. (Prov. 22:6)

Fathers, do not provoke your children to anger by the way you treat them. Rather, bring them up with the discipline and instruction that comes from the Lord. (Eph. 6:4)

The Numbers Don't Lie

Throughout Scripture, God clearly explains that He has given parents the privilege and responsibility of shaping their kids' spiritual lives. It was not and is not God's plan for parents to bring their kids to church a couple of times each month and assume the children's ministry will take care of their spiritual development.

The numbers simply don't work: Even if your child attends an hour-long program at church every week, that's only fifty-two hours a year—and most families don't attend every week. In fact, the definition of "regular church attendance" has changed so much in the past decades that the term currently applies to some of those who go to church fewer than half of the Sundays in a year.[4] The reasons for the decline in attendance are many and varied: children's sports teams often schedule games on Sundays; more parents have disposable income and take their families on trips or to a second home; and inspiring church services are available on television or online.

Quite often, children want to participate in church activities, but the parents have other priorities. I'll never forget the child who desperately wanted to be a part of a summer ministry event, but his dad refused because it would cut into his son's baseball practices. The boy was ready to choose growing in his relationship with God over baseball, but his father was more concerned about his batting average than his spiritual growth.

Perhaps you're not one of those parents. Maybe you make sure your child attends both church and the youth group to benefit from a dedicated children's ministry team that works hard at developing resources, planning lessons, and creating an atmosphere where your child will learn, worship, and draw closer to God while developing strong relationships with other young Christians. I applaud your commitment! But this scenario has a problem: it still only covers two hours a week, or 104 hours a year. The paid professionals and volunteers in church ministries, no matter how excellent they are, can't give your children all they need to live a strong, effective Christian life in only two hours a week. Moses, Solomon, and Paul all knew that!

Parents have an average of more than seventy waking hours each week with their children. That's 3,640 hours a year—not including their time at school and sleeping. Of course, many kids are involved in extracurricular activities, but those are things we choose; they're not required. And parents may not actually use the seventy hours each week to connect to their kids in meaningful ways, but the time is there.

Charles Spurgeon was one of the greatest preachers of the 19th century. He was known for his brilliant insights into the Scriptures and his powerful application of spiritual truth to individuals' lives. In his book, *Spiritual Parenting*, he wrote,

> Children must be fed. They must be well fed, or instructed, because they are in danger of having their cravings perversely satisfied with error. The only way to keep chaff out of the child's cup is to fill it brimful with good wheat. The more the young are taught, the better; it will keep them from being misled.[5]

The truth is that leading children in their spiritual development is one of the greatest joys in life.

Pouring ourselves into young lives isn't a grind. Far from it! The truth is that leading children in their spiritual development is one of the greatest joys in life.

When my daughter Ashton was a little girl, Cherith and I began reading the Bible to her and praying with her. She asked lots of questions, and we had wonderful conversations. Then, one night, it happened. I was praying with Ashton before she went to sleep. She looked up at me and said, "Daddy, can I ask Jesus into my heart?"

I asked her what she thought that meant. Her answers showed me she definitely understood God's love and forgiveness, so I led my daughter in the prayer of salvation.

It was an unbelievable experience! Cherith and I celebrated the amazing born-again experience of our daughter. I was on cloud nine! Over the next several days, I told everyone about God giving me the privilege of leading my own daughter to the Lord. I was present for the most important moment in my child's life. It was one of the greatest joys of my life!

So now when parents bring a child to me and ask me to lead him to Jesus, I explain the joyous opportunity they might be missing. I give them some pointers about how they can talk to their child about Jesus and pray together. I want to equip and inspire you, as well, to have meaningful spiritual conversations with your kids, your grandkids, or your nieces and nephews.

1. "Spiritual growth" is a topic for many conversations, not just one.

Remember, Moses told the people to talk with their kids about God "when you sit at home and when you walk along the road, when you lie down and when you get up." Don't wait until you think your kids are "old enough" to talk to them about God. Their training starts from the moment they're born (or even earlier, in the womb). Talk to them about God's grace, His love, His mercy, His provision, and His purpose for their lives. Talk on their level, but talk!

Moses mentions "when you lie down and when you get up." I think those are crucial moments in our daily schedules. Right before bed is a perfect time to stop, talk to your kids, and pray with them.

My kids know that every night before bed, Cherith and I will stop whatever we're doing to pray with them about the day they just had. In the morning, we don't try to talk and pray with them as soon as they get up. I'm not sure if the reason is that they're not coherent at that time of the morning, or if I'm not coherent. Either way, it doesn't work for us. Instead, we use the drive to school as an opportunity to have good conversations. Rather than cranking up the radio or an MP3, my kids and I use our morning commute as a time to memorize Scripture and quiz each other.

Those two times work in our family, but you have to find the times that work best for you and your kids. You don't have to follow my example or the model of any other parent—but you need to find something that works! Regular spiritual conversations are crucial. We all need to hear spiritual truth many times and from several different perspectives. Have you ever wondered why the New Testament contains four Gospels? Wasn't one story of the life, death, and resurrection of Jesus enough? They all say the same thing, don't they? Well, yes and no. Each one approaches the same eternal truth from a different angle. We need to hear and read and understand all of them to get a clear picture of the nature of Jesus Christ. In the same way, all of us— parents and kids alike—need many conversations about the gospel and the gospel's impact to help us understand salvation and our new motivation to obey God. Many rich and varied conversations show your kids that God is the center of your family and permeates everything you do.

2. Share what you know.

Don't feel like you need a Bible college degree before you start talking to your kids about God. Share what you already know—and believe it or not, you probably know a lot! Tell what you know to be true about God and His love.

> **Don't feel like you need a Bible college degree before you start talking to your kids about God.**

Talk about what it was like for you to become a Christian. Review what you learned in church on Sunday. Describe what God showed you as you read your Bible this morning. No matter where you are on your own spiritual journey, you have plenty to share with your kids.

3. Learn more so you can share more.

Don't take the lazy route. Be a *disciple*, which means "student" or "learner." Spend time with God daily, and read His Word. When your kids see that you are passionate about God and Scripture, your example will be a catalyst for many conversations about what matters most to you: God, His love, and His will for your life.

Paradoxically, the more you know, the more you realize how much you don't know. That's not a bad thing . . . unless it intimidates you. As you learn more, your questions will multiply. If you aren't sure about something, ask someone.

Not long ago I received an email from a dad. He wrote, "I have questions about how to talk to my son about baptism. He showed an interest in getting baptized this past Sunday after church. Where should I begin?"

I was thrilled to get his message! Notice that he didn't ask, "Can I make an appointment for you to explain baptism to my son?" He asked, "How do I talk to him?" I was most eager to help.

The more you learn, the more you can share with your child . . . and you'll be a resource to help other parents learn to talk to their kids, too.

4. Pray daily with your kids.

It's a good thing to pray at meals, but pray more often than that. Pray when they leave for school, when they go to bed, and when you or they face a difficult choice. Let prayer become part of the fabric of your family's life.

You don't have to pray grand, long prayers that sound like a preacher: "O Jehovah, I beseech thee on behalf of my offspring . . ." Let your prayers be simple, honest, and heartfelt. Prayer is simply talking to God and allowing Him to speak to you. That's the kind of prayer kids appreciate, and it's the kind they are far more likely to emulate. As your kids see how much you value prayer, it will increasingly become part of their daily lives, too.

When you pray with your kids regularly, you never know what kinds of opportunities will arise for meaningful spiritual conversations. Melody Jones told me a story about her daughter, Morgan. They pray every day while driving to school. One morning Morgan asked if they could pray for her to learn a lot about Jesus at school that day. But there was a problem: Morgan didn't go to a Christian school. Melody told her, "We can't pray you will learn a lot about Jesus at school today because they aren't allowed to teach you about Jesus."

Morgan thought for a moment, and then she simply adjusted her prayer. She prayed, "God, help me to teach people at this school about You. I want to be a missionary to my school."

That morning in a conversation about prayer and school, Morgan had a major revelation about what it means to share the love of Jesus with her friends. All of that happened because Melody made daily prayer with Morgan a priority.

5. *Have regular family devotions with your kids.*

Just as regular conversations and prayer with your children should be simple and natural, so should family devotions. Gather your family together, read a passage in the Bible, and discuss what it means. Elevate the importance of the Bible. One of the core values for our church, our children's ministry, and our family is: "The Bible tells us about God and His grace. It's our guidebook for living."

I suspect that many parents read the previous paragraph, throw up their hands, and moan, "Well, great. That's a lot of help. My Bible has over 2,000 pages. Where do I find a passage that makes sense to me?"

Don't despair, and by all means, don't give up! You can find plenty of really good resources to use if you need them. Find some that work well for you and your family, and dive in! You may run across some questions that challenge you and your children. Don't be shocked. Use the opportunity to say, "I don't know the answer to that. I'm going to find out. We'll talk about it again when I have some answers."

Every family has a different rhythm. Maybe the best thing is for your family to have family devotions on Tuesday night, or maybe it's Saturday morning. Find a regular time you and your family can take a timeout from the busy schedule of life to talk about God, the Bible, and what each of you are learning. (For downloadable instructions and a sample of family devotions, go to www.briandollar.com and click on *Talk Now and Later*. You'll find this resource and many others.)

6. Worship with your kids.

Kids need to see their parents praising God and responding to Him with honesty, joy, and gratitude. When a parent is excited about worshiping God, it's contagious. Many churches don't provide a time when the whole family, including babies and toddlers, come together to worship. I understand that little kids (and sometimes bigger kids) can be disruptive, but all children need to see, hear, and feel a worship experience with their parents. I know it's inconvenient for many people, but it needs to happen sometime, somewhere, somehow.

Of course, worship isn't restricted to church buildings. We can make it a part of our family devotions and everyday life at home.

7. Serve with your kids.

One of the ways to teach our children *about* God is to do things with them *for* God. Every community and most churches have plenty of organizations and ministries that are family-friendly. No, you're probably not going to take your children to work with addicts and prostitutes, and you're not going into crack houses to share the love of Jesus there. Those ministries are important, but they're for adults.

One of the ways to teach our children *about* God is to do things with them *for* God.

Ministry is about using your gifts, talents, time, and abilities to serve God and others. God created you for a purpose and gifted you and your kids for a reason: to use your gifts for His kingdom. The opportunities to make a difference in your church and community are almost limitless. Here are some examples of opportunities to connect your family with others in meaningful ways:

- Serve with your older kids in your church's nursery or children's ministry.

- Work with an organization that feeds the homeless.

- Participate in a clothing drive for a women's and children's shelter.

- Invite an exchange student to live with you.

- Work on a Habitat for Humanity housing project.

- Usher at church together.

- Organize a singing group to go to nursing homes.

- Serve in the resource room for a crisis pregnancy center.

- Identify disadvantaged people in your community and serve them by doing work in the yard, painting, or cleaning.

- Serve in the community food pantry.

Take advantage of opportunities for your whole family to serve together in ministry. It's effective, it's appreciated, and it's fun.

Serving together opens many doors for spiritual conversations. Almost invariably, the exposure to the real needs in people's lives brings up a lot of questions: What happened to them? Why do they need our help? How long have they been like this? How long will it last? Who else is helping them? What's the future for them? How can we pray for them? Every person in the family should be involved in ministry somewhere!

A heart for God is more often caught than taught. Allow your kids to see the heart of Jesus in you as you serve together. Serving together may make more of a difference in their openness to God than anything else you can do. Don't miss this golden opportunity!

8. Model godly behavior for your kids.

Too many moms and dads subscribe to the erroneous philosophy: "Do as I say, not as I do." This is, not to put too fine a point on it, a disaster! This approach abdicates the God-given responsibility to be an example your kids want to follow. Modeling is far more powerful than verbal instruction as a teaching tool. What we do speaks far more loudly than our words, especially if our actions and words are inconsistent! Rarely will children have higher moral standards, higher academic standards, higher relational standards, and a higher sense of purpose than their parents.

In *Nurturing the Leader within Your Child,* Dr. Tim Elmore asserts:

> Perhaps the best exercise for you, as a parent, is to ask yourself: What leadership qualities and skills do I naturally model? These you will pass on whether you try to or not. Your kids will catch your lifestyle. Next, ask: Which leadership qualities and skills do I lack but need to possess because they are so critical for my child to learn? We teach what we know, but we reproduce what we are.[6]

Modeling is far more powerful than verbal instruction as a teaching tool.

Similarly, it's sobering but essential to ask yourself, "Will my children be drawn closer to God if they pattern their life after my . . .

- entertainment choices?"

- vocabulary?"

- reactions to those who hurt me?"

- acceptance of those who are different from me (ethnically, racially, economically, etc.)?"

- compassion for the lost?"

If you want to have meaningful spiritual conversations with your kids, make sure your actions don't invalidate your words; model godly behavior for your kids.

9. Allow your kids to ask questions.

Kids ask questions . . . plenty of questions. It's what kids do. I know it wears you out and makes you tired, but their curiosity is a good thing. When kids ask questions, it opens the door for spiritual conversation and growth. Encourage their questions, celebrate them, and ask for more.

Several friends shared some of the questions their kids have asked.

Lori said, "My kids understand God created the universe, but they always want to know, 'Who created God?'"

Brenda said, "My son asked me why we should pray for things since God already knows what's going to happen before we were even born."

Jenny's daughter asked, "Why does God let bad things happen to good people?"

These are excellent and very difficult questions.

I know what you're thinking, "What if my kid asks me a question about the rapture or whether or not our dead cat is going to be in heaven?" Don't panic. Here's the answer . . .

10. Don't be afraid to say, "I don't know."

It might be a blow to your ego to actually admit you don't have the answer to a question your kids ask, but don't worry. It won't destroy your kids' confidence in your parenting skills. Actually, it's healthy for you to admit to your children that you don't know something, because then you can . . .

11. Discover the answer together.

Make your search for the answer an adventure. Look it up in the Bible together. As a family, discover what God's Word says. If you're still stumped, ask a pastor or other spiritual leader about it, or ask another parent whose kids are a little older and probably asked the same question.

Not knowing isn't the end of the world. In fact, it's a wonderful thing for the kids to see you excited about finding what the Bible says about a particular subject. You're showing them that exploring the Bible for answers to tough questions is normal . . . exciting . . . and worth the effort.

However, don't assume there's a simple, right answer to every question. For centuries, brilliant Bible scholars have debated some very difficult issues. Especially with older kids, it may be helpful to explain different (even opposing) positions and let the differences become fuel for wonderful discussions.

12. Explain the gospel in clear, understandable terms.

Please don't misunderstand me. I'm not suggesting you "dumb down" the gospel message. Jesus said all of us—kids and adults alike—are to become like children in order to enter the kingdom of heaven (Matt. 18:2–4).

On the other hand, don't assume your child isn't ready when he or she shows a desire to trust in Christ. I've known parents who wouldn't let their children receive Christ or be baptized because the children couldn't explain the theology well enough to suit the parents. They make the decision for their child: "Nope! Now is not the time for you to accept Jesus! You just don't understand it well enough."

When you explain the gospel to your child, use simple, clear terms.

A certain level of theology is crucial, but only enough to tap into the marvelous truth of God's amazing grace. I haven't seen a particular point when all children have the ability to grasp the message of God's forgiveness through Christ. Every kid is different, so be ready to explain it and offer an opportunity to receive Christ.

When you explain the gospel to your child, use simple, clear terms. Don't talk like a biblical philosopher, trying to sound really smart. Jesus didn't. He used parables and stories to help people understand biblical truth.

- When He was in a farming community, He talked about how the kingdom of God was like a farmer sowing seed.

- When He was with fishermen, He compared living for God to "fishing for people."

- With a woman who had gone to a well, He offered "living water."

- To connect with anyone and everyone, Jesus explained that He was—and is—the source of true nourishment, safety, and hope. He said, "I am the bread of life," "the light of the world," "the gate for the sheep," "the good shepherd," "the resurrection and the life," and "the true vine."

People understood what Jesus said. He used everyday language and common objects to illustrate the gospel message and make it come alive for the listener.

Jesus found ways to connect the heart of God with each person He met. But today we have many different and practical methods we can use to present the gospel. I want to walk you through a very simple method I have used thousands of times to explain the gospel to kids. It's called "the bridge." All I need is a blank sheet of paper and a pen.

It starts at the beginning. I draw two plateaus (out West, they call them mesas), with a deep chasm between them.

God created the first people (Adam and Eve) and placed them in the Garden of Eden where everything was perfect. They enjoyed a close relationship with God. Sadly, one day Adam and Eve decided to disobey God and eat of the fruit that God had commanded them not to eat. When we disobey God, that's called sin. Sin is bad behavior, but it's more than that; bad behavior shows that we want to run our lives without God. That's what caused Adam and Eve to disobey God—they wanted to run their lives apart from Him. When the first sin was committed, something terrible took place.

Suddenly, humankind was separated from God. The separation didn't apply only to Adam and Eve, but to everyone who followed them as well. In Romans 3:23, Paul explained, "For everyone has sinned." That means you, me, and *everyone*. And because of sin, Paul told us in Romans 6:23, "The wages [or payment] of sin is death."

Death is separation from life. In other words, sin caused us to be separated from eternal life—the love, joy, peace, and purpose God had planned for us. Now people are on one side, dying in their sin. God and His eternal life are on the other side. And there's a problem: People can't get to God because of sin. The payment for sin has to be made by someone, either us or someone else—but who?

God had a solution.

In John 3:16, Jesus tells us what God did to remedy the problem: "For this is how God loved the world: He gave his one and only Son, so that everyone who believes in him will not perish but have eternal life."

Jesus came to earth and died on the cross to pay the price for our sin. Because of Jesus, we don't have to pay for our sins because He paid the price for us.

Because Jesus died and rose again, He created a bridge we can cross to get to God. How do we do that? First John 1:9 tells us: "If we confess our sins to him, he is faithful and just to forgive us our sins and to cleanse us from all wickedness."

When we accept what Jesus did on the cross and ask His forgiveness for our sins, we are no longer separated from God. We are brought back together with Him. He welcomes us into His family, and we will live forever with Him in heaven! That's His promise!

That's the message I share with children, but it works just as well with teenagers and adults. In fact, it was originally developed by an organization called The Navigators that shares the gospel with adults. You don't have to memorize a hundred passages of Scripture and study theology to explain the gospel to a child. God wasn't trying to make it hard to understand. His truth is plain and simple. God loves you! God loves every child! God has a plan for every man, woman, boy, and girl to be in relationship with Him!

There are two kinds of good news here. The gospel of forgiveness and eternal life is the good news that changes lives, but it's also wonderful news that God wants to use you—a parent, a grandfather or grandmother, an uncle or aunt, or another loving adult—to be the primary spiritual influence in the life of the child(ren) you love. When our hearts are melted and molded by the love of God, and when we're amazed that Jesus would willingly—even gladly— give His life to pay for our sins and make us His own, talking about the gospel isn't a chore. The love of God pours out of us because Jesus has poured His love into us . . . and His love changes everything, for us and for our kids.

It's important to remember that your child's response isn't up to you. We can't make someone else believe. Our task is to be as loving and clear as possible, and then leave the results to God. In any conversation about God, there's always another person present: God Himself! Before we talk to kids about God, it's wise to talk to God about our kids. Here's my prayer for them and for you.

> Father, thank You for the precious children You have put in our care. We love them and we realize You love them even more. We ask You to open their hearts to understand the wonder of Your love, forgiveness, and acceptance. Use us to make it clear, and use Your Spirit to open little hearts and minds to grasp the truth. We ask, Lord, that these children will grow strong in their faith and become mighty warriors in Your kingdom! Continue to use us, Lord, to guide them, to correct them, and to love them every step of the way. In the wonderful name of Jesus, Amen.

Now, you're ready. You can do it!

chapter 2

How to Talk to Your Kids About Death and Tragedy

When we experience a sudden calamity or a long, drawn-out illness and death, our natural instinct is to ask questions: "Why?" "How could this happen?" "God, where were You?" It's no surprise, then, when our kids ask the same penetrating questions.

No family, church, or community escapes tragic loss, which often happens when we least expect it. One of the main roles of pastors and other leaders is to show up during those times and comfort people who are shaken and are grieving. It's also the role of parents to be there to comfort their kids, answer their questions as best we can, and help them grieve in a way that produces strength and tenderness instead of resentment. It's a tough job for pastors, and it's equally tough for parents.

In one tumultuous week, our church family suffered a couple of tragedies. A young woman—a loving wife and mother who served in our children's ministry—died of brain cancer. The children adored her and were devastated. Their parents struggled to find satisfying answers for their children's hard questions. Many parents called me to ask if they should bring their young children to the memorial service. That's a hard call. For some kids it might be too much, while others would benefit from the opportunity to express their grief with others in the church family.

The woman's death wasn't the only heartache that week. A tornado devastated several neighboring communities, resulting in several other deaths and many instances where survivors lost everything they owned. Some of the people in our church knew the victims and mobilized to attend to them, and we cared for people we had never met before as well. Devastation knows no boundaries, and our love knows no restrictions.

The kids' questions about the deaths, injuries, and wreckage from the storms were similar to their questions about the lady who died of brain cancer: "Why did God let this happen?" "When will it happen again?" "Do you think it will happen to our family?"

Tragic events are burned into our memories. I remember exactly where I was the day the Columbine massacre was announced. As the facts became clear, we all discovered that two students, Eric Harris and Dylan Klebold, walked into their school heavily armed and murdered twelve students and a teacher. Their gunfire wounded twenty-one more, and then they took their own lives. I couldn't believe the news. I had never seen that kind of devastation and tragedy on a school campus. Yet years later, I again remember exactly where I was the moment I learned of the horrific tragedy in Newtown, Connecticut. Again, a deranged young man walked into a school—this time, an elementary school—and killed twenty little children and six teachers who were trying to protect them. I was shocked at the death toll and rocked by the devastation. One crazed young man ended the lives and stole the futures of so many innocent children and loving adults. It just didn't make sense. It still doesn't make sense.

Perhaps you remember the thoughts that went through your mind on those horrific days or when you learned about a devastating natural disaster. You might have thought, *Wow! That could have happened in my city. It could happen to someone in my family!* It's true. Tragedy doesn't discriminate between races, classes, or religions. It can hit any community, any family, or any individual at any time.

After the school shootings, especially the one at Sandy Hook Elementary School, many parents tried to shield their very young children from seeing the news or hearing reports about the events. They didn't want to terrify their kids. Parents of older children couldn't keep the news from them, yet they struggled to find words to explain this kind of degenerate and evil behavior. I understand. I had difficulty explaining it to Ashton and Jordan.

Apart from newsworthy disasters (mass shootings, terrorist attacks, plane crashes, earthquakes, and so forth) that have an effect on everyone, all families have other specific personal tragedies: the death of a loved one, an accident that permanently injures someone, the sudden loss of income due to layoffs or being fired, a prolonged disease, dementia in an elderly relative, divorce, or even the death of a pet. These are the everyday losses that parents struggle to explain to their kids.

Parents reasonably wonder:

- How much do I tell my kids?

- Do I tell them everything is fine when it isn't?

- What kind of assurances can I give them?

- Do I allow them to be a part of family discussions about difficult matters?

- Do I let them go to the funeral?

- Should I let them look at the body in the casket?

- How do I handle their questions about death?

- Should I initiate conversations about their feelings and perceptions, or should I wait for them to bring it up?

These are all legitimate but difficult questions. As a kids' pastor, I'm often asked to help children who are grieving or struggling to deal with loss. I'm not a psychologist, but I've had a lot of experience . . . more than I ever wanted. In addition, I've been a sidelines observer watching parents, grandparents, aunts, and uncles care for children through extremely difficult times. As I have watched, I've seen some bizarre methods people have employed in attempting to help their children deal with grief.

All of us need to help our children face heartache, grieve productively, and learn important lessons as they encounter the inevitable tragedies of loss, but not all of us are equally skilled in this effort. Some people have a God-given ability to read young people and empathize with them. Others are, to put it charitably, not so gifted. They don't seem to connect with others on an emotional level, and they often offer simplistic advice that hurts more than it helps. I'm not sure whose example they follow or where they get their information. It seems like they get it from heavy metal rock lyrics or a horror movie. Wherever it comes from, it's bad . . . really bad.

Hollywood can produce some touching, helpful films, but others are anything but therapeutic. In the movie *Hugo*, the main character is a boy who lives alone in a bus station in London. At one point his mind flashes back to the day his dad died. Hugo expects his father to come get him, but instead, his uncle bursts into the room looking worried. Hugo asks him, "Where's my dad?" His uncle breaks the news of his dad's death to Hugo by taking a long drag on his cigarette, exhaling, and saying, "Your dad's dead. Now, pack your bags and come with me."

That's not the best approach.

Obviously a family may experience a wide range of losses. We could try to identify degrees of pain or types of loss, but the concepts of compassion, grief, and healing overlap all of them. Therefore, we'll look at the principles that guide us as we help children cope with any kind of loss. You can tailor the principles to fit the particular heartache your child experiences.

Don't ignore events that aren't a big deal to you but are traumatic for your child.

Don't ignore events that aren't a big deal to you but are traumatic for your child. For example, you may not be particularly attached to a pet, but your son or daughter may be devastated by the pet's death. Sometimes it seems the connection a child has with a pet is even stronger than some human relationships. For kids and their beloved pets, the loss is just as deep, and grief is just as necessary. Be patient, understanding, and engaged.

A child's capacity to understand and cope with death—and your approach to discussing it—will vary according to the child's age. Each child is unique, but here are some guidelines.

1. Be honest.

This advice may sound unnecessary, but it's essential. You might say, "Of course, I'll be honest. Why would I lie to my child?" I'm not talking about telling blatant falsehoods; I'm referring to the tendency of many parents to give seemingly benign statements meant to soften the hard news but that actually confuse the child.

I've heard well-intentioned parents say things like, "Grandma just went on a long trip. We will see her in heaven one day," or, "Uncle Jerry is just asleep." A clinical psychologist told me that one mother told her seven year old that his dad was away at college rather than let him know his dad was in alcohol rehab. Unfortunately, this isn't an isolated instance.

Many parents naturally want to protect their children from emotional pain, but distortion and disinformation eventually create more pain because the child realizes he can't trust the person who was supposed to tell him the truth—even the hard truth. The problem is that some parents underestimate their kids. Most children are bright and sensitive. They see through false information and wonder why you didn't trust them with the truth. Lies, however well intentioned, short-circuit the healing process and prevent the child from developing effective coping strategies for future tragedies and losses.

Parents don't want their kids to hurt, but they're short-sighted about how benign deceit will affect them. I suspect that many of those parents experienced traumatic events in their past, didn't fully grieve and heal from them, and now want to protect their children from similar distress.

I believe kids are capable of handling tragedy. Given the truth, support, and time, they'll find a way to work through it and come out stronger. When parents communicate confidence in their children's emotional strength and assure them that God is there to help, they raise kids who are less fearful and more capable, who learn how to handle life's inevitable heartbreaks and tragedies.

2. Use appropriate language.

I mean more than, "Don't cuss." Speak directly and avoid words and phrases that might confuse the child's thinking. Until kids are about five or six years old, their view of the world is literal, so explain sickness, tragedy, or death in concrete terms. For example, you may have to explain that "dying" or "dead" means that the body stopped working. If someone dies who was ill or elderly, you can explain that the person's body wasn't working anymore and the doctors couldn't fix it. If someone dies suddenly in an accident, you can describe the event (without too many details) and say that because of this sad event, the person's body stopped working.

Young kids often have a hard time understanding that all people and living things eventually die, that death is final, and they won't come back in that body again. Even after you've explained it as well as you can, and perhaps several times, young kids may continue to ask where the loved one is or when the person is returning. As frustrating as this can be, continue to calmly reiterate that the person has died and can't come back into his or her body.

Avoid using euphemisms such as telling kids that the loved one "went away," "went to sleep," or even that your family "lost" the person. Because young kids think so literally, those kinds of phrases may inadvertently make them afraid to go to sleep or fearful whenever someone leaves the house. Think on their terms and communicate on their level.

Kids from the ages of about six to ten are usually capable of grasping the finality of death, even if they aren't fully prepared to deal with the fact that it will happen to every living thing. At this age, they often connect cause and effect, but they may get it wrong. For instance, a nine year old might think if she behaves, says a prayer, or makes a wish, grandma won't die. Also, kids at this age often personify death as the "boogeyman," a ghost, a skeleton, or the grim reaper. They deal best with death when given accurate, simple, clear, and honest explanations about what happened.

Help them understand that death is something the Bible teaches will happen to all of us. It's a natural part of life. The writer of Hebrews makes clear that each person is destined to die once, after which comes judgment and salvation for God's people (Heb. 9:27–28).

3. Allow them to ask questions.

When we're honest with kids, they naturally ask a lot of questions. You can answer some of them very easily, but some questions have no easy answers . . . and some have no answers at all, at least not in this life. Whether the questions are elementary or require a PhD in philosophy and theology, create a comfortable, open atmosphere. Send the message, "There's no right or wrong way to feel." When kids feel safe, the conversations can be rich and wonderful, even if the topic is tragedy, illness, or death.

> **When kids feel safe, the conversations can be rich and wonderful, even if the topic is tragedy, illness, or death.**

You may be afraid of questions because you don't have all the answers. This moment in the life of a family is a crucial time for love and support. Don't be anxious about not knowing all the answers. Treat each question with respect, and help the child find his or her own answers. Use God's

Word as a guide. Talk to someone who has been in a similar situation before. With input and prayer, explore the answers with your child.

As children's understanding about death evolves, questions naturally arise about mortality and vulnerability. They connect the dots and wonder, "What if *that* happens to me?" For example, if a friend dies in a car accident, they might be reluctant to get in a car. The best way to respond is to empathize about how frightening and sad the accident was. It's also a good time to remind your child about ways to stay safe, like making sure to always wear a seatbelt and never get in a car with a driver who has been drinking.

Dr. Susan Bryant told me how she handled the Newtown tragedy with her son Michael, who was eight at the time:

> When Michael heard about the Connecticut school shooting, he had a lot of questions. I told him in a matter of fact way that bad things happen, and the odds were very low of it happening here. I told him that I choose to believe he's safe when he goes to school, and I'm going to trust God to help me handle whatever happens. Because I wasn't very worried about it, he decided not to be worried. Michael is not a terribly anxious child. If a parent has a very anxious child, it's wise to give these neutral responses and remind the child he or she can handle the unknown. I tell parents to never tell a child that something bad won't happen when there is a chance it might.

I always emphasize that *if* something bad happens, kids need to know they can handle it. I say, "I may not know *how* I'll handle it, but I *know* I'll handle it. It may not be pretty to watch, but I'll get through it somehow."

4. Allow your child to be emotional.

Don't stifle your child's emotions. Let children express hurt, fear, anger, and confusion. Too often, fathers (and many mothers as well) feel uncomfortable with expressions of emotions and tell the child to stop! For the child, this compounds the loss. When children are crying over the loss of a loved one, telling them they need to "be strong" or "toughen up" cheapens the life of the one they're mourning. It signals to the child, "This person wasn't worth that kind of emotional reaction." It also sends the message, "Emotions are threatening! Stuff them!"

King David cried when his son Absalom was killed. Mary and Martha cried over Lazarus, and Jesus wept at the tomb. The Psalms express many powerful emotions, including the full range from joy to anger, gratitude to grief. Allow children to feel the full depth of their pain and emotions, and remember that God invites you to feel your pain, too. Sorrow can seem overwhelming, yet if we are honest enough to face it, the pain gradually subsides and joy returns. Solomon explained,

> For everything there is a season,
> a time for every activity under heaven.
> A time to be born and a time to die.

A time to plant and a time to harvest.
A time to kill and a time to heal.
A time to tear down and a time to build up.
A time to cry and a time to laugh.
A time to grieve and a time to dance. (Eccl. 3:1–4)

5. Be aware of your own need to grieve.

I tell parents that focusing on the children in your care is important, but not at the expense of your own emotional needs. Adults who have lost a loved one will be much better able to help their children work through grief if they too are in the process of grieving.

Crying is necessary. It cleanses the soul, it's an emotional release, and it's the appropriate and necessary reaction to significant loss. Some form of weeping is the right way to grieve the pain we feel when we lose someone we love. Emotions can make us feel out of control, but a psychologist wisely observed, "You can't heal what you can't feel."[7]

There's a time for tears, and it doesn't make you any less of a person . . . not even less of a man. Jesus wept, and He was the strongest, bravest man who ever lived.

When parents are honest about their own pain, they become more approachable, understanding, and compassionate. Then they can invite their children to grieve with them.

6. Grieve together.

Grieve as a family. Share the tragedy and the emotional reaction to the tragedy. God has wired us in such a way that

we need others to share loss with us. Paul reminded the Roman
believers, "Be happy with those who are happy, and weep with
those who weep" (Rom. 12:15). We should weep with others
and share their sorrow. Grieving together is perhaps the most
powerful and recuperative part of the healing process.

**Grieving together is perhaps the most powerful
and recuperative part of the healing process.**

The Bible provides both positive and negative examples
of this principle. On the positive side, we see Jesus grieving
with Mary and Martha when their brother Lazarus died. At
the other extreme, we read of Job who had the worst day ever
recorded. In a single day, he lost almost everything—his servants, his livestock, and even his children. He suffered from
painful, ugly boils. His wife was still around, but she wasn't
much help. Her advice was, "Curse God and die" (Job 2:9).

The Bible says that Job sat on a pile of ashes scraping the
boils on his skin with broken jars. That's about as bad as it
gets. Upon hearing the news, Job's three friends came to be
with him. The writer describes the painful scene:

> When three of Job's friends heard of the tragedy he
> had suffered, they got together and traveled from their
> homes to comfort and console him. Their names were
> Eliphaz the Temanite, Bildad the Shuhite, and Zophar

the Naamathite. When they saw Job from a distance, they scarcely recognized him. Wailing loudly, they tore their robes and threw dust into the air over their heads to show their grief. Then they sat on the ground with him for seven days and nights. No one said a word to Job, for they saw that his suffering was too great for words. (Job 2:11–13)

When they first arrived, Job's visitors were exemplary friends—they didn't give advice or blame anyone. They just sat and grieved with him. But they couldn't leave well enough alone. They believed Job must have sinned to cause God to send such a calamity into his life. Most of the rest of the book of Job is a discussion, sometimes pretty heated, between Job and his friends. As it turned out, they weren't real friends at all. Job then had compounded problems: the loss of almost everything he had, feeling abandoned by God, and now false accusations from men he trusted!

The New Testament describes another missed opportunity for people to come to the aid of someone who was suffering. When Jesus was in the Garden of Gethsemane the night before He was crucified, He asked Peter, James, and John to pray with Him. Jesus wanted to know someone was there for Him. But His three closest friends went to sleep while Jesus prayed so earnestly that His sweat fell like great drops of blood! His friends weren't there for Him when He needed them (Luke 22:39–46).

The point is that we need each other. Family members can help each other find comfort and a new sense of purpose during times of suffering. As children get older, they can grieve over tragedies with more understanding. Older kids can be a great comfort to their parents when the whole family suffers loss.

Sometimes a grandparent, uncle, or aunt can step into a child's life to provide additional support and comfort—for the child and the child's parents. If your child feels close to an extended family member, ask that person to play a significant role in the grieving process for your child.

When a tragedy hits your family, don't go off by yourself and grieve. Grieve *for* your loved one, and grieve *with* your kids. Grieve as a family. Hold each other, listen to each other, and allow people to be emotional without "fixing," stuffing emotions, or judging.

Allow your child to be emotional, but let me offer a word of caution . . .

7. *Don't force an emotional response.*

Let emotions come, even if they seem disproportionate to the event. However, some kids turn inward to keep from feeling and/or expressing their emotions. Hurt, fear, and anger are too uncomfortable, too threatening, so they stuff them deep inside. When you sense this is happening, talk about the loss you feel, but don't ever try to coax children to respond in a particular way. That will only make them more defensive and reserved. If you remain honest and appropriately vulnerable, your child may let down her guard and begin to express the feelings that are buried deep in her heart.

People grieve in different ways. Some are loud and demonstrative, while others are quiet and reflective. Your way may be very different from your child's. Don't think that the child *must* cry at certain times or in particular ways in order to grieve the loss. I've seen parents push and prod their children to cry when tragedy strikes. They say things that produce shame instead of emotional honesty, such as, "Don't you miss Grandma? Why aren't you crying?"

Some parents gather their kids together at the casket and begin to sob. If a child in the group isn't crying, or isn't crying loudly enough, a parent may stare at him through sobbing eyes with an inquisitive (and manipulative) expression. It makes the child feel very uncomfortable.

To complicate the family dynamics during a time of loss, some children display their grief with outbursts of anger and disobedience. Don't be alarmed, and don't be too quick to punish. Let the child know that you, too, feel upset about the tragedy or death. A child who acts out in this way doesn't know how to express sadness. To him, anger seems more normal and natural. Take time to teach, to model, and to comfort. Recognize the anger as a cry for help, not an act of defiance against you.

Allow children to process the loss in their way and at their pace. Often, a death may not even "hit" the child until weeks later. Watch your expectations, and provide plenty of grace to everyone in the family. Treat their responses with respect, and give them the room and support to grieve in their own way.

8. Expect regression.

In the wake of loss or a tragic event, many children regress and engage in behaviors from their early childhood, particularly ones that are associated with comfort, such as playing with favorite toys or wanting to sleep in the same room with their parents. These behaviors are normal coping mechanisms in the face of tragedy and aren't a cause for alarm. Most children return to more age-appropriate behaviors within a month or two of the event, and often sooner. However, if these behaviors continue beyond two months, consult your pediatrician. Particular attention should be paid to regressive behaviors that interfere with your child's functioning, such as refusing to go to school or refusing sleep or food.

9. Pray together.

Remind children that we have a God who loves us and wants to help us through the pain and loss. To some extent, virtually everyone who grieves feels abandoned, so they need to be reminded that they are not alone. God hasn't failed us, and He hasn't forgotten us. The writer to the

Hebrews assures us, "For God has said, 'I will never fail you. I will never abandon you'" (Heb. 13:5).

The parents are the spiritual leaders of the family and should model for other members the importance of praying *for* one another and *with* one another. Gather everyone together and ask God to give you comfort, strength, love, and patience as you face the pain of loss. Allow the Holy Spirit to be the Comforter, as Jesus identified Him (John 14:26, KJV). The Spirit whispers His love, comforts us in our pain, and gives us guidance to take the next steps.

As the Holy Spirit brings comfort, He touches the hearts of parents and children with assurance of His presence and purposes. Sooner or later, the sorrow fades and we experience a deeper confidence in God. We develop the kind of faith Gregory of Nyssa saw in Basil: "ambidextrous faith"—welcoming pleasures with the right hand and difficulties with the left, convinced that God will use both to accomplish His purposes.[8]

Every child needs to know that suffering can produce this kind of strong faith—and every parent needs to know it, too. Our children need to hear us articulate our confidence that God is loving, powerful, and kind, and that He will give us wisdom and strength to face the heartache and come out stronger. In fact, the parent's response to tragedy—faith or doubt, honesty or denial, patience or impatience—is a key factor in the child's development.

10. Remember that grieving is a process, not an event.

Some people see others struggle in the grieving process, and they callously comment, "Why don't they just get over it? It's been a month now!" One good cry isn't the end of grief; it may be only the beginning. Grief is unpredictable, messy, and uncomfortable for both parents and children, but it's absolutely necessary if we are to grow stronger and wiser from our loss. Children need time to process the hurt, to sort through all the emotions, and to learn valuable lessons about love and life. For parents, it's important to *stay engaged* no matter how long it takes.

The Question of Suicide

Sadly, suicide doesn't always happen to *those other* people or in *that other* family. It can happen in any community and in families where you would never expect it. A recent study by the Centers for Disease Control reports that more people are dying from suicide than car accidents.[9]

From time to time, parents ask me how to talk to their kids about a suicide in their family or their community. Some people may believe that suicide is the "unpardonable sin" and feel justified in condemning the person and assigning him or her to hell. Yet when this tragedy touches them and their families, their theology often suddenly shifts to grace.

That's the strange aspect of our nature. When it comes to us, we want mercy; when it comes to someone else, judgment.

Certainly, suicide isn't God's design, but neither is *any* sin, including the exaggerations I use when I want someone to think I'm cool. Sin is sin, but some sins are far more devastating than others. In such cases, I want to offer grace, peace, and comfort to the hurting and trust that in His grace, God will comfort those who are devastated by the loss. I don't presume to make any pronouncement about the person's eternal destiny. That, too, is in God's hands.

Stages of Grief

Experts who study the grieving process have identified at least five stages. These stages aren't necessarily a linear process. People may go through two or three, then take a step back and start over again. And most people go through several complete cycles of grief, going deeper each time. The five stages of grief[10] include:

Denial (or numbness)

Denial is when a person simply refuses to accept what has occurred. Someone may say, "My father can't have cancer. He was just fine last week!" "A car wreck! No, it can't be her! My daughter couldn't have been in the car. There's no way!" "No, she's not an addict. She really needs those pills. She has been in such pain."

Denial can take many forms, ranging from literal disbe-
lief to emotional shutdown, which makes it appear as if the
person isn't affected by the loss. Those are self-defense mea-
sures, designed to protect the person from experiencing the
full intensity of the loss. Instances of denial and numbness
may alternate with brief periods when the person acknowledges what happened, its implications, and the feelings that
come with it.

Anger

Some Christians believe all anger is sin, and they refuse
to admit they are ever angry. This misunderstanding can be
a significant problem in normal times, but it's devastating
during the deep disruption of catastrophic loss. The *feeling* of
anger isn't sin. Our *expressions* of anger can certainly be sinful if they are designed to exact revenge in any way, or they
can be noble if they motivate us to protect the innocent. Paul
describes the right balance in his letter to the Ephesians:
"And 'don't sin by letting anger control you.' Don't let the
sun go down while you are still angry, for anger gives a foot-
hold to the devil" (Eph. 4:26–27).

If people believe all feelings of anger are wrong, they will
be stuck in this stage indefinitely. At some point, everyone
who experiences loss feels a deep sense of injustice and gets
angry because "it doesn't make sense." People who experience the death or disability of a loved one, for example, may
get intensely angry at that person for abandoning them or

for causing them pain and financial instability. Some may get angry with themselves for "allowing" something bad to happen, even though they had no control over it. Anger makes some people feel more powerful, more in control. It's preferable to the deep, overwhelming, debilitating feelings of helplessness.

The healthy—and godly—approach to the stage of anger is to be honest with God and with at least one other person about internal, intense emotions. Being honest about the emotions lets us be honest about the loss, and both are essential in the grieving process.

Bargaining

When the anger begins to subside, the person usually tries to find another way to deal with the situation. She tries to make a deal with God. She may say to herself, *If I promise God I'll give a lot of money to the church . . . or better, directly to the poor . . . then He will surely answer my prayers and cure my mom of cancer.* Or a child might think, *If I pray real hard and promise to be a missionary, will God bring my dog back?*

Essentially, the person going through the grief still refuses to accept reality and begins to believe there might be ways to reverse what has happened through his own actions. It is a form of denial. To a degree, the person accepts what has happened, but he doesn't believe it's final. He hopes he can still make a deal with God and turn things around.

Sadness (or depression)

Sooner or later, all the attempts to make a bargain with God are exhausted, but God hasn't bought into the deal. The reality of the loss and its implications eventually become undeniable, often months after the tragic event. At this point, people are overwhelmed with deep, pervasive sadness, a condition that looks and feels a lot like the symptoms of depression. They may not want to get out of bed, they don't want to eat or they eat too much, they have trouble sleeping or they sleep too much, they don't enjoy the things that used to bring them pleasure, and they may completely withdraw from normal social interactions.

The difference is that the grief stage of sadness is a necessary step toward wisdom, strength, and healing. A *temporary* withdrawal from external events and responsibilities can be beneficial to provide time to reorganize their emotional life to match their new reality. Ongoing depression, however, only leads deeper into the pit of despair.

Unfortunately, people in this stage often can't see any light at the end of the tunnel. They need a friend, a mentor, a pastor, or a counselor to see them thorough this crucial stage and help them come out on the other side.

Acceptance

At some point, people who have been going through the process of grieving will be able to integrate the impact and the meaning of the loss into their lives. The event itself and all the feelings and reactions attached to it become part of the person's "redemptive life-story." The pain of the loss and wisdom learned through grief take their appropriate places alongside other significant experiences in life. However, this does not mean the person is "done" with the loss and can move on as if it never happened. It simply means that it no longer dominates the mental and emotional landscape as much.

> **At some point, people who have been going through the process of grieving will be able to integrate the impact and the meaning of the loss into their lives.**

Where Are You? Where's Your Child?

Virtually every person gets "stuck" sometime, somewhere in the stages of grief, usually multiple times at different stages and in different ways. The most common points of blockage are denial and bargaining, but people can get stuck anywhere at any time.

How long, then, does it take to grieve? Great question. The answer is that it varies according to many factors: the closeness of the relationship, the sensitivity of the one who feels the loss, any other recent losses that compound the pain, and the presence or absence of support during the grieving process. Most people have unrealistic expectations about how long it will take. They expect to "get over it" within weeks or months, and they're shocked when they still suffer flashbacks, anger, and periods of crying long after the death or traumatic event.

We would like to think that we can move swiftly through the process, but those who try to rush it inevitably short-circuit the process. This doesn't mean the person cries for two straight years, but it takes a long time to process the pain and learn the lessons God wants us to learn. Yet we don't have to wait to start learning these lessons. We can begin gaining insights, wisdom, and strength as we move out of the bargaining stage.

Some might hear about the slow pace of grieving and insist, "Yes, but I'll trust in God, and He will get me through it a lot sooner." Certainly, God's love and strength give us courage to keep going forward through the painful process, but His grace keeps us *on* the path. He seldom *speeds up* the pace.

When you or your child feel stuck in grieving—angry, sad, or hopeless—it's hard to make good decisions. In these times it's wise to seek help from a professional counselor.

If you're worried as to whether or not your child is "stuck" in the grieving process after many months have passed since the event, here are a few signs to look for:

- She spends an inordinate amount of her time thinking about the loss, even to the point of ignoring daily responsibilities.

- He feels sad, hopeless, or angry most of the time.

- She loses interest in things or people she used to enjoy.

- He doesn't want to talk about the person or the event . . . ever, to anyone.

- She feels guilty that she is still alive, or she feels guilty for being happy, as if she is betraying the deceased loved one.

But don't be surprised if your child or grandchild moves through the grieving process much quicker than you do. Kids are extremely resilient. Although a year seems like a blink of an eye to an adult, it's an eternity in the life of a child. While it may seem that your kids are moving too quickly, give them room to process things at their own speed in their own way. If you see any warning signs, have a conversation with your child and talk to your pediatrician or counselor. Even then, your child may be doing just fine. Be observant, be wise, and be gracious.

It can be confusing—and frustrating—for a parent who is still grieving to see that the child has moved on. Many parents presume their kid's progress will mirror their own, but that's seldom the case.

Becoming Channels of Grace

We often think of the apostle Paul as a tough guy. He was certainly courageous as he suffered, but he appreciated comfort just as the rest of us do. And he received enough comfort from God to share with others in need. In the opening of his second letter to the Corinthians, he explained,

> God is our merciful Father and the source of all comfort. He comforts us in all our troubles so that we can comfort others. When they are troubled, we will be able to give them the same comfort God has given us. For the more we suffer for Christ, the more God will shower us with his comfort through Christ. (2 Cor. 1:3–5)

Grief has enormous potential to teach us life's most important lessons, but it threatens us to the core. If we refuse to undergo the grieving process, we become either numb or hardened. Either way, we lose the ability to give and receive love, and we miss out on the treasure trove of wisdom God has for us "in the darkness." Patiently going through the various stages of grief requires great courage, but if we endure, we will have more compassion, insights, and love than ever before. Only those who have been deeply hurt and have completed the grieving process can effectively comfort another person who has suffered the pain of tragic loss.

I often recommend a resource to help parents and children walk through the process of grieving. The material is adapted from Yvonne Butler Clark's *It's Okay to Cry*. To download this resource, go to www.briandollar.com and click on *Talk Now and Later*.

Chapter 3

How to Talk to Your Kids About Sex

You may have turned to this chapter of the book for many different reasons: your kids may be asking questions about sex; you may be afraid they'll ask questions about sex, or perhaps you're just curious about what a children's pastor recommends for the most intimate and challenging communication between parents and their kids. Whatever your reason may be for reading this chapter, pay close attention—you and your kids need to get this right!

The mere thought of talking to children about sex makes many parents feel uncomfortable . . . *very* uncomfortable.

When I gave this talk to parents at our church, the look on their faces was both heartwarming and amusing. Some parents squirmed and shifted in their seats during the whole presentation, and others sat like stone monuments. Some looked terrified, but all were curious. For several parents, especially those who grew up in conservative churches and silent families, the idea that a pastor would actually address the subject of sex goes against everything they've ever assumed, thought, or believed!

Many parents (and some pastors) are convinced that the subject of sex has no place in any part of church life. It's off limits, taboo, unmentionable. This would be news to the writers of the Bible. They seemed to think the topic was important—so important that it should be addressed with a blend of sensitivity, boldness, awe, and delight. The assumption that the subject of sex is off limits fails to grasp a crucial biblical concept.

God Created Sex

Sex is a beautiful gift, created by God for the purpose of giving a husband and wife an intimate, physical way of expressing love for one another. Every act of sex renews and deepens the marriage covenant the couple made to fully belong to one another.

I don't know where the church got the idea sex is somehow dirty and a topic Christians should never talk about. I guess they haven't read their Bibles. In the opening chapters that give the account of creation, Adam was alone. God caused him to fall into a deep sleep, and He formed Eve out of one of Adam's ribs. Don't miss the next scene. A naked man sees a naked woman, and he's so thrilled that he bursts out in a rapturous love song: "At last! . . . This one is bone from my bone, and flesh from my flesh" (Gen. 2:23)!

That's how the Bible starts, but the topic of sex doesn't end there. Song of Solomon is an entire book of the Bible devoted to a poetic (and graphic) depiction of the delights of sex for a married couple. The imagery describes the couple in a state of arousal. Yes, that's in the Bible too! (I suspect that at this point a lot of readers are putting this book down and discovering that Bible reading is more interesting than they ever imagined!)

Of course, God instituted sex as the means for the human race to reproduce. God gave the first couple instructions that must have been a delight to hear and obey: "Be fruitful and multiply. Fill the earth and govern it. Reign over the fish in the sea, the birds in the sky, and all the animals that scurry along the ground" (Gen. 1:28).

When a person insists that sex shouldn't be mentioned in the church, we can conclude that he or she hasn't read the Bible (or has read it with blinders on). The subject isn't just found in the opening chapters of Genesis and one obscure book in the Old Testament. We can find it throughout the Bible, where the topic of sex is addressed more than one hundred times!

The church has been silent on this issue for too long. For centuries, children (and adults) who attended church heard little to nothing on the subject of healthy sexuality. Perhaps the Puritans were afraid of the subject, or maybe Queen Victoria's famous reticence shaped our spiritual culture. (She was too embarrassed to call parts of a roasted chicken "breast" and "leg," so she called them "white meat" and "dark meat.") In the 1960s, the sexual revolution in America caused the church to recoil in horror. These and other factors have made many Christians feel uncomfortable talking about sex.

Pastors haven't been bold to address the subject, and their silence has reinforced the misperception that Christians should never let the topic touch their lips. Sadly, the only time some kids and teens hear about sex in church, the message is negative: "Don't have sex! It's dangerous, so stay away!"

The disparity between the church's silence and pervasive sex in every other part of modern life is confusing, especially to kids.

Negative messages, silence, discomfort, and misunderstanding have formed a vicious cycle of ignorance in the church. In the meantime, secular culture has become saturated with images, songs, and talk about sex. The disparity between the church's silence and pervasive sex in every other part of modern life is confusing, especially to kids. It's time we did something to break the silence. It's time to speak openly and appropriately about this wonderful gift from God.

Christians of all ages need to hear the good news: sex isn't bad; it's good. In fact, it's *very* good. God designed it. It's His idea and His gift to us.

Few Parents Give Their Kids a Healthy Sex Education

However, there's a big problem in many Christian homes. I asked a large group of parents at our church, "How many of you received healthy, value-centered sex education from your parents when you were growing up?" Some replied that their parents gave them a book (a lame book) or tried to have as short a conversation as possible, which was more confusing than enlightening. Very few of their own parents provided a relaxed, informative, comprehensive, Bible-centered series of conversations about the nature of sex.

Many of today's parents have told me their parents never attempted to give them *any* information about sex. They probably assumed their kids would learn all they needed to know from their friends or in the backseat of a car. Our parents didn't talk to us about healthy sexuality, and unfortunately, we're not doing much better with our own children. A vast majority of young people say they receive more information about sexuality from their friends, media, and school than from their parents. This is not good news, especially when all studies show that the more positive, value-centered sex education kids receive in their home, the less promiscuous they will be.

Many adults feel uncomfortable discussing sex with anyone, much less impressionable kids! Instead of wading in to tackle this vital subject, they make excuses, such as:

"My child is far too young to even approach the topic."

"My kid won't listen when I try to talk about anything important. I'm sure it would be the same with sex."

"I don't have to worry. My child would never have sex before marriage!"

"I don't need to talk about oral sex with my child. It's far too odd and too rare to even mention."

The only one of these statements that might be valid is that small children may be "too young," but even then, we need to be ready to answer their questions when they ask.

Many parents (and even more, grandparents) have heard myths about sex and have accepted them as truth. One of the biggest myths is: "If I tell my kids about sex, they're more likely to have sex." They're paranoid about their kids becoming sexually active. They foolishly think that by postponing discussing sex for as long as possible, they'll somehow keep children from learning about it and committing sexual sin. Typically, today's parents are more aware and more committed to doing a better job of communicating with their kids, but too many well-meaning moms and dads are remaining silent for too long.

In addition, many parents are afraid that talking about sex will rob their children of their sexual innocence, or they're afraid their children's sexual desires might be awakened far too early. The typical mindset of a Christian parent is: "If I talk to them about sex, it will make them more curious. And there's no telling where curiosity may lead!" Because sexual activity is off limits for our kids' behavior, we've made it off limits for our conversations with them.

The best person to teach your children about sexuality and relationships is you!

Some parents avoid bringing up the subject from fear that the kids might ask about *their* experiences, and they aren't proud of how they handled their early sexuality. Those fears and doubts may be very real, but they shouldn't be excuses to remain silent. The best person to teach your children about sexuality and relationships is you!

The fact is that our children *are* going to learn about sex. They may find out from television or movies, from the

Internet, or from their friends (who, as we know from our own adolescence, are rarely paragons of truth!). When I think back on the conversations I had with my friends when I was a boy, I have to laugh. Talk about misinformation! Other kids aren't a trustworthy source of truth about sex. Parents are.

Don't you want to be the one who gives them accurate information and a biblical view of the beauty and sacredness of sex? It's far better for them to learn it from a reliable, loving source early in their lives than to wait, get information from dubious sources, and experiment to find out more. The world's culture has cheapened sex, but God's view of sexuality is wonderful and magnificent.

Cherith and I decided we didn't want our kids to learn about sex from the playground or from the movies. We didn't want our kids' first exposure and understanding about sex to be a distorted view shaped by ignorant and excitable kids or graphic and untamed images on the screen. We didn't even want the school Sex Ed class to be where they first learned about it. We wanted our kids to learn about sex from us.

When we relegate sex education to the science teacher at school, we abdicate our God-given responsibility. It's not the role of the school system, public or private, to teach morals and values, and it definitely shouldn't be left to the latest pop star!

Cherith and I had a full and comprehensive conversation with Ashton when she was in the fifth grade, but decided to talk with Jordan a year earlier. Why the difference? Boys tend to discuss sexual things at an earlier age, and we didn't want to have to correct things he learned from his friends. We wanted him to get a proper perspective from us from the beginning.

Was it easy? Not exactly. One of the main reasons parents don't talk with their kids about sex is because they're uncomfortable *and* the kids are uncomfortable—which makes for a very awkward conversation. Cherith and I were prepared, and we pressed through it. When we described sexual intercourse in specific detail, the responses of Ashton and Jordan were hilarious. Ashton covered her face and couldn't stop giggling. In the moment, we didn't try to correct her or get her to react in a different way. Instead, we acknowledged that we understood it seemed funny to her, but we reiterated how beautiful it was that God created such an intimate way for parents to express their love for each other and build their families. After a while, though, she began asking questions and discussing all kinds of aspects of sex—without embarrassment or hesitation. It was wonderful!

Jordan, on the other hand, had a completely different reaction. In the midst of the conversation he was dialed in, hanging on every word. When I said, "The husband places his penis into the woman's vagina," he blurted out, "No, he doesn't!"

Cherith tenderly assured him, "Yes, he really does."

Jordan again insisted, "No, he does *not!*"

Cherith and I nodded, and this time I told him, "Yes, son, he does."

Jordan paused for a moment, and then asked, "Why would he do that?"

The first time I taught parents how to talk to their kids about sex, Jordan was about ten. The day before my talk, I jokingly said I wanted him to go with me and explain how he had reacted when Cherith and I first talked to him about sex. I often kid with Ashton and Jordan, so I figured he knew I wasn't serious. Instead, he thought for a second and then asked, "Dad, can I bring some notes to use when I talk?" He was ready! (Obviously, I would never do that to him.)

Principles and Practices

As you think, pray, and prepare to talk to your children about this important topic, consider these guidelines:

Begin early.

The time to initiate this conversation may be earlier than you think. In today's society children are exposed to information about sex at an extremely early age. As hard as we try to shield our kids from sexually explicit (and even implicit) movies and magazines, it's almost impossible to completely screen out those images and messages in our sex-saturated culture. Don't let the media do your job for you. Make sure you're giving your children the correct information!

How early is early enough? I recommend teaching healthy sexuality as early as possible. When children are toddlers, begin teaching them about their sexual organ. Teach them that it is special and should be kept private, not shared with others. And teach them that they shouldn't allow others to touch them in an inappropriate way.

When kids are in early elementary grades, they'll probably begin asking questions about how they were born. Don't lie to them about a stork. Teach them about the beauty of creation. Mothers might explain, "God grew you in my tummy for nine months, and then you were born."

Inevitably, children ask, "How did I get out of your tummy?"

Don't make something up. Tell them the truth. You might say, "God planned for babies to come out of their mommy's vagina."

Some mothers have looked shocked and told me, "I don't want to tell them they came out of my vagina! That will disturb them." When I asked those parents how they explained childbirth to their kids, some of them said their mothers told them, "Mommy pooped you out."

Really? Do those parents actually think that's *less* disturbing to a child?

Use proper terms instead of nicknames for body parts.

Don't call your son's penis a "wee-wee." Don't call your daughter's vagina a "woo-woo." From their earliest childhood, use the correct terms. We don't use strange names for other body parts, like knee, ankle, or stomach, so giving nicknames to genitalia or bodily functions implies that the real words are secret or dirty. When we make up nicknames for sexual organs or functions, kids draw conclusions: those parts of their bodies are shameful and bad; they and their parents shouldn't discuss such things because they're too private to talk about; and their parents feel too uncomfortable to have these conversations.

When parents use the proper names for genitalia and bodily functions, they send the message to their children that sexuality is good and natural. They also communicate that they're willing to talk openly and honestly and will remain nonjudgmental about any questions that are asked. This underlying message of honesty and openness is crucial—for this topic and for every other meaningful conversation between parents and their kids.

As your kids mature, increase the amount of information you give.

Remember that sexual information (like all important topics) is like baggage. Only give young people what they are able carry.

Remember that sexual information (like all important topics) is like baggage. Only give young people what they are able carry. Add more when they can handle it. Start early, but be wise in how much information you give your kids. Don't give every detail of sexual intercourse to a four year old. A child that age isn't able to process the information. Instead talk about how boys and girls are created differently, and that's why we practice modesty.

My suggestion for what to share at what age is this:

- Ages one to nine: Protect their innocence. Answer their questions but don't give them ideas. (Many parents never move past this stage. They keep protecting their kids when the children are teenagers and young adults!)

- Ages ten to eleven: Have "the talk" with your child.

- Ages twelve and up: Listen more and talk less. Keep communication lines open.

Talk about God as the Creator.

As your kids grow older, they'll ask you about the specifics of how they were made. Stress the point that God created each part of them. He created their eyes, ears, brain, as well as their penis or vagina—and He has a specific purpose for each body part. You might share King David's outburst of wonder at God's creativity. He prayed to God, "Oh yes, you shaped me first inside, then out; you formed me in my mother's womb" (Ps. 139:13, *The Message*).

When children reach the elementary school years, begin to talk about things in a general sense without going into details and specifics. For instance, a parent might explain,

> "When mommies and daddies show love to each other, sometimes they hug, kiss, and hold each other. Did you know that when Mom and Dad hold each other, their bodies fit together in a special way, and sperm from Daddy's body enters Mommy's body? God combined Daddy's sperm with an egg in Mommy's body, and you were created. The reason you look like Mom and Dad is because we both played a special part in creating you!"

It's perfectly fine to say that there's more to the story, and that you will share the rest of it with them when they're a little older.

Schedule "the talk."

When your child reaches the age that you feel he or she is ready to hear more details about the act of sexual intercourse and God's purpose for it, do your homework. Talk with your spouse (or the child's other parent), and find out if the other adult would like to be a part of the process. Often, this adds another layer of embarrassment, so many parents find yet another excuse to put off this important discussion with their child. Procrastination may be understandable, but it's not helpful. The longer you postpone giving your children accurate information about sex, the more likely they'll get misinformation from another source.

Put it on the calendar. Tell yourself, "This is the day and time I'm going to have the conversation." Don't put it off, and don't let anything interfere. Be the adult. Schedule the talk, and then prepare for it.

Create a comfortable and safe environment to talk.

Don't spring details about intercourse on a child in the middle of dinner or when someone else can hear the conversation. Turn off the television, minimize distractions, and find a place where your child feels comfortable. For some, sitting in the living room or at the dinner table is the best environment. Others may prefer an outdoor walk and talk. Don't let the conversation be hurried. Block out a couple hours just in case your child has a lot of questions. If possible, schedule a day or a weekend getaway with your child to have plenty of opportunities to talk, relax, and come back to talk more.

Relax.

You may feel nervous as the time for the talk approaches, but remind yourself that you're doing something wonderful for your child—something that will pay dividends for the rest of his or her life! It's a good idea to script and rehearse your opening line. This preparation will give you confidence.

As you begin, be aware of your body language. If you appear uptight, your child will sense your discomfort. Sit back, open your arms, and smile. Tell your child you're going to talk about something wonderful . . . because you are! And then dive in. You'll probably be amazed at the wonder and thrill you and your child have as you talk about sex as a gift from God.

> **You'll probably be amazed at the wonder and thrill you and your child have as you talk about sex as a gift from God.**

Keep God as the focus.

Continually remind your child that God created sexual intercourse. As you describe the actions involved, remind your child that sex is God's plan for a husband and wife to express love to each other. Also, it's the way He designed for them to have children. Yes, there are specific movements and interactions, but sex is also a beautiful and mysterious blessing between a man and wife who are committed to one another. Paul explained to the Corinthians, "There's more to sex than mere skin on skin. Sex is as much spiritual mystery as physical fact. As written in Scripture, 'The two become one'" (1 Cor. 6:16, *The Message*).

If you prefer, use additional resources or illustrations.

You may find it helpful to use books, videos, or illustrations to help your child understand the intricacies of sex. Not every child is an auditory learner. Some children need more than their parents' verbal descriptions for them to comprehend the act and meaning of sex.

Illustrations are helpful for children, but be sure your resources only include simple drawings rather than detailed illustrations or photographs. You can even find pop-up books that allow the illustrations to be three-dimensional. This makes it easier to explain about body parts and sex in a way that young children understand.

Cherith and I found a video online that was a computer-generated animation of sperm traveling through a vagina, finding the egg, and fertilizing it. The video then shows a rapid transformation of a baby as it grows to full term. We found this to be an especially helpful tool for our kids.

Emphasize that God has reserved sexual intercourse for marriage.

The Bible is clear—and we need to be equally clear—that God designed sex to be a beautiful and meaningful expression of love, but He reserved it for married couples. Sex is not a casual way of expressing love to someone of the opposite gender. It's an important part of the covenant a couple makes with God. Every act of sexual contact is a sign of the covenant and a covenant renewal ceremony. Sex, then, is an intimate act that God wants us to honor by keeping it between a man and wife only. The writer to the Hebrews explains, "Honor marriage, and guard the sacredness of sexual intimacy between wife and husband. God draws a firm line against casual and illicit sex" (Heb. 13:4, *The Message*).

Explain that sex is a component of a healthy, committed relationship—not a stand-alone event.

Near the end of our major sex talk with Ashton, she asked something that helped us realize our explanation hadn't been clear. She said, "So, you guys have had sex two times already?"

We explained that a woman doesn't automatically get pregnant every time she and her husband have sex. She thought for a couple of seconds, and then she asked, "Well, how many times have you guys had sex?"

I answered, "Not as many times as Daddy would like!" (I'm just kidding! I would never tell my kids something like that . . . even if it's true!)

Allow your child to ask questions.

Be honest and answer your child's questions—all of them. Don't freak out, and don't make fun of anything you might be asked. That's the surest way to shut off communication.

> **Be honest and answer your child's questions —all of them.**

If your children ask a question you feel would be better answered when they're older, then let them know that. You can say something simple like, "That's a great question, but I think you'll understand the answer better in a year or two. Let's wait until then. In the meantime, please ask anything else you want to ask."

Many times kids ask the same questions over and over again. You may think you've answered them, but your explanations may have gone over their heads, or they may have been preoccupied with a previous part of the discussion. Even though sex is a very interesting topic, kids sometimes simply forget what we've told them, or our explanations may conflict with other input they've gotten from their friends, and they're confused. Welcome any and all questions, even the ones you've answered a dozen times! When children repeat questions, wise parents use the opportunity to remind them of the importance of relying on information received at home, not on playground wisdom.

Encourage your child to keep conversations about sex between you and them.

We told Ashton and Jordan that it's very important for children to hear about the wonders of sex from their parents, not from other kids. Although their curiosity about their friends' level of understanding is understandable, we asked them not to share what we've told them with others.

All parents deserve the opportunity to share this information with their children. Tell your child that parents might choose to talk to their kids about sex at different times and in different ways. Ask your child to respect the parents of their friends enough not to share information they've learned.

On the other hand, there's no reason to become alarmed if your child reports having conversations about sex with others in his or her class. These conversations are entirely normal. If you've talked with your child openly and honestly about sex, without embarrassment, he'll probably report his playground discussions to you.

One of the things to watch out for, however, is when older kids talk to your child about sex. Quite often, older kids use talk about sex to impress young ones . . . or worse, to manipulate them.

We encouraged our kids to share with us what others have said to them, especially if they're confused or concerned. We've assured them that we will *always* tell them the truth. When they've heard some random comment about sex from an older child or they've seen something in a movie, they can come and ask us about it. We'll make things clear for them.

Invite your children into an ongoing conversation.

Let your kids know you want an open dialogue with them about sex. Explain that there are many sources that give them incorrect and unbiblical information. Let them know you will periodically bring up the subject and initiate conversations to keep the subject of sex a natural topic to discuss as a family.

As your kids move into preadolescence, begin initiating conversations with them about how their bodies are going to change. Help them be prepared when it happens. Moms, talk with your girls about menstruation, hygiene, and sexual boundaries with the opposite sex.

Dads, talk with your sons about masturbation, wet dreams, oral sex, establishing and respecting sexual boundaries, and treating girls with honor and respect.

Don't shy away from the tough issues. Discuss lust, sexual temptation, peer pressure, homosexuality, and everything else. Nothing is off the table. Treat each subject with respect and reverence. Have *real* conversations about *real* subjects.

Remember the goal: a lifetime of sexual integrity.

Many parents have the wrong purpose when they think about their kids and sex. Their goal is to do everything possible to make sure their child stays pure until his or her wedding day. That's not a bad goal, but it's not the primary one. I believe it's more important for parents to instill God's purpose for sex. When the goal is avoidance, the kids hear only "Don't!" But when the goal is delight in marriage, the child hears, "When you follow God's design, sex is more wonderful than you can imagine!" There's a difference . . . a big difference.

Helping children establish lasting sexual integrity starts at a young age and extends throughout their lives. It shapes their self-concept, guides how they treat members of the opposite sex, maximizes joy and intimacy in marriage, and gives them the desire to remain faithful in mind and body.

We have no difficulty teaching our children healthy eating habits. We certainly want them to eat their broccoli, whole grain breads, and other good things while living at home. More than anything, though, we want them to continue reaping and enjoying the benefits of eating healthy after they've moved out.

Similarly, a core commitment to sexual integrity doesn't come from a one-time conversation or a sex education class. It develops as parents instruct, discuss, and model a life of Bible-centered sexuality. When I talk with young people who have grown up with sexual integrity, they usually mention having ongoing conversations with their parents that, at least most of the time, felt natural. No matter their age, kids learn best when they talk and dialogue, not when parents just lecture.

Invite God into the Conversation

Talking to kids about sex is a spiritual experience. We trust God to give us wisdom, compassion, and clarity. We need Him to help us understand the way kids think and process information at every stage of development. As we prepare to talk to them about sex, we pray and ask for His insights, blessing, and courage. As we talk, we may need to pray to know the next words to say to answer a hard question. And as we continue to open lines of communication with our kids, we thank Him for the privilege of seeing our kids pursue truth and learn to walk in God's light.

Talk to God *about* your conversations with your kids about sex, and talk to God *with* your children about sex. God isn't embarrassed. After all, it was His idea!

Chapter 4

How to Talk to Your Kids About Self-Image

In our Information Age, we're bombarded with messages all day long—from television, magazines, radio, online sites, texts, and other people. We receive these messages at home, in the car, at work, on the Internet, and practically everywhere we go. Our culture is message-saturated. If anything, our kids receive even more messages than we do!

According to the Yankelovich Consumer Research quoted in the *New York Times,* the average person sees between 3,000 and 20,000 marketing messages every day. The higher figure includes every conceivable viewing of advertising, including the labels of every product we pass at the grocery store or vending machines.[11]

The average teenager sends 3,339 texts a month, which is more than six every hour they are awake. Girls, on average, send 4,050. A Nielsen survey shows an 8 percent increase in only one year.[12]

All of these messages affect our kids, our grandkids, and us in a number of ways, both positively and negatively. If you think you're impervious to the power of these messages, think again. They're the water we swim through every day. Like a fish can't avoid getting wet, we can't avoid the deluge of messages—and all the advertising works! We buy those products and use those services. They influence our priorities, purchasing decisions, and lifestyle choices. They shape our expectations and our identity. To a great extent, the messages we receive every day define who we are, what we believe, what we do, and where we're going in life.

Let's think about our kids. We might separate the messages they receive into four categories: negative, manipulative, purposeful, and gracious.

Negative messages scream or whisper: "You're not good enough." "You'll never amount to anything." "You're stupid." "You're too fat (or too slow or too short or too ugly)." What makes these messages more damaging is that they often come from parents, teachers, friends, or the mirror. For some who send these messages, hurting others is a sport, but more often the messages are designed to crush the child's spirit to make him or her more compliant.

Manipulative messages promise love, acceptance, success, comfort, or thrills—but always with strings attached. The person has to jump through hoops to be accepted. Advertising is inherently manipulative. There's always a promise beneath the promise—the toothpaste promises to clean your teeth, but what the ad is really selling is the promise that whiter teeth will give you the acceptance, love, and friendship you crave.

Purposeful messages point people to a higher goal and a more significant meaning in life. Parents, teachers, coaches, and friends can encourage young people to find and follow their purpose in life. Of course, Christians have a higher and deeper sense of purpose: to know, love, and serve God in all we do.

Gracious messages communicate unconditional—and in fact, *counter-conditional*, because they are the opposite of what people deserve—love. Everyone is flawed, and we all need to be forgiven, restored, and believed in. This is the message every person on the planet longs to hear: "I love you no matter what, and there's nothing you can do to alter that!"

I think many parents would be stunned to live in their child's skin for a day and experience the negative and manipulative messages they see and hear. Our kids desperately need us to communicate purposeful and gracious messages to them—sincerely, tenderly, boldly, and consistently—especially when they've lost hope and experienced criticism and failure. To some degree, their present sense of security and hope depends on the messages we give them, and their future even more so.

> **I think many parents would be stunned to live in their child's skin for a day and experience the negative and manipulative messages they see and hear.**

There are many reasons why kids (of any age) may have a negative self-concept. Let's look a little deeper at some of the factors that slowly erode or suddenly crush a child's sense of security and significance.

1. Poisonous Messages

As we've seen, destructive, hurtful messages can come from peers, teachers, parents, or society in general. Kids hear a barrage of negative messages every day telling them that they aren't handsome or pretty enough, smart enough, or cool enough to fit in. And it often only takes *one* negative statement to affect a child for a very long time. Like a knife wound, it can happen in an instant, but it heals slowly . . . and not at all if the person suffers more wounds.

My friend David Richards told me that when he was eight years old, he overheard two of his aunts having a conversation. They had no idea he was listening. One of them said, "That David is such a smart aleck. He gets on my nerves so much!"

His aunt's words stung him like a hornet. David is now seventy years old. He told me, "I still remember that day like it was yesterday. The pain of that one statement has stayed with me for sixty-two years."

The messages we give our kids are almost always shaped by the messages our parents communicated to us. Our hearts are filled with those messages, whether negative, manipulative, purposeful, or gracious—and "out of the abundance of the heart the mouth speaks" (Matt. 12:34, NKJV). If you're having a hard time communicating positive messages to your child, you may need to be honest about the messages you've internalized. Only then can you grieve and heal past wounds, and then change your present words and actions.

You may have grown up in a home where there was rarely any praise or affirmation. Perhaps your drill-sergeant father rode you all the time. Your childhood was filled with statements like:

"Why can't you ever do anything right?"

"Why do you always mess everything up?"

"You'll never amount to anything!"

"I wish you'd never been born!"

Your self-esteem is low because one of the most significant people in your life constantly tore you down and criticized you. It might have been a parent, a sibling, or a spouse. For years, they blamed, belittled, and criticized you. Over time (and it didn't take long), you internalized it and began to believe it. Another person's comments and criticism became your picture of yourself—your worth and your identity.

My friend Lori grew up in a poor family. When she was a child, she was ridiculed because she never had the "right kind" of clothes to wear. She was called names because she was poor. It took years for her to get over those destructive messages. No matter how nicely she dressed, she just never believed she measured up to others' expectations.

William grew up with an alcoholic father who was physically present but emotionally absent. His mother lived with a barely controlled fury that her life wasn't turning out the way she hoped. William remembers, "I walked on eggshells every day. My dad's only message to me was, 'You don't matter enough to me for me to pay attention to you,' but my mother was a different story. I lived to avoid her anger, so I did everything I could to please her. To her, nothing I ever did was good enough. I'm sure she was primarily angry at my father, but when I was a boy, it sure felt like I was the main target!"

Poisonous messages are powerful and destructive. The people speaking them may or may not know they are ruining someone's life. Either way, they crush the person's soul.

We've all heard the old saying, "Sticks and stones may break my bones, but words will never hurt me." What a lie! Negative messages can devastate us—and our kids. If you've been the recipient of such messages, don't be surprised if they spill out in your relationship with your kids. But do something about them!

2. Comparison

We easily recognize negative comparison as destructive, but positive comparison is also hurtful. When a parent, teacher, or peer tells a child, "You're prettier, smarter, or more this or that than another person," the not-so-subtle message is, "You're on thin ice! One false move and you'll be the target of criticism!"

Comparison is inherently manipulative. Parents may think they're properly motivating a child by using comparison, but it produces pride, shame, or fear in the child—pride when they compare favorably, shame when they don't, and fear that they may try and still fall short. When kids are the targets of negative or positive comparison, they become insecure, which results in being driven to succeed or becoming passive because of fear.

When we measure our self-worth, talents, accomplishments, possessions, or strengths against someone else, we'll eventually come out on the bottom. The problem with the comparison game is that we can *always* find someone who is better than we are. In *Mere Christianity*, C. S. Lewis observed,

> Pride is *essentially* competitive—is competitive by its very nature—while the other vices are competitive only, so to speak, by accident. Pride gets no pleasure out of having something, only out of having more of it than the next man. We say that people are proud of being rich, or clever, or good-looking, but they are not. They are proud of being richer, or cleverer, or better looking than others. If everyone else became equally rich, or clever, or good-looking there would be nothing to be proud about. It is the comparison that makes you proud, the pleasure of being above the rest.[13]

We can play the comparison game in any area of life. We may be thrilled for the moment when we feel like we're winning, but it always leaves us empty. Wealth, possessions, degrees, lavish vacations, the latest technology, beauty, second homes, and everything else promise ultimate fulfillment, but they can't deliver because someone else always has a little bit more. The problem with comparing to others is that whether you win or lose at the moment, you always lose in the end.

As parents, we need to be aware of how much we play the comparison game with our peers and how much we use it to "motivate" our kids. We also need to find a new way to communicate with them.

3. Abuse

There are many different types and degrees of abuse. People may have suffered sexual, physical, or emotional trauma, from mild to severe. Some encounters leave bruises and scars; others leave no visible sign. One type of wound many don't consider "abuse" is physical or emotional abandonment. In these cases victims avoid angry faces, bitter words, and horrific encounters, yet they're left with a gaping hole in their hearts.

Many children have been hurt by people they trusted. The pain is so severe it makes them feel as if they aren't "normal" or "valuable." They begin to blame themselves for what happened, even though it wasn't their fault. Trauma causes children to respond in many different ways. Some become hardened and are determined never to trust anyone again. Others become dependent on others, especially those who abused them. Children (and adults) who suffer abuse may try to find love through promiscuity. They may try to numb the pain with drugs or alcohol. They may engage in compulsive behaviors to try to control something (anything!) in their lives.

Victims of abuse can't just "snap out of it." They need plenty of love, understanding, and time to heal the wounds of a broken heart.

Shaping and Reshaping a Child's Self-Concept

Many factors can damage the heart of a child. The disruption of divorce, disease, moving to another city, an absent parent, financial pressures, and other problems can affect a child—especially if several are present and have a cumulative impact. It's easy for a parent to feel helpless when it comes to forming a child's self-esteem. Some have told me, "There are so many voices speaking into my child's life—outside forces that I have no control over. How can I positively affect my child's self-esteem?"

Your child's self-image is being formed from the day he or she is born. The messages you send matter! Children's self-esteem is shaped by the significant people in their lives. Parents, of course, play the most important role because they have countless opportunities to steer the development of the self-esteem of a child or teenager in a positive direction. But don't overlook the impact a grandparent, uncle, or aunt can have in speaking powerful messages of encouragement, hope, and value into your child.

As a parent or grandparent, your messages need to fit the age of the child, his or her personality, your personality, your way of parenting, cultural influences, economic conditions, and many more factors. Let me offer some principles that can help every parent.

1. Help children see themselves the way God sees them.
One of the main reasons people view themselves as worthless is because they don't see themselves from God's

vantage point. They've listened to what others say about them—or they're afraid others think they're worthless or incompetent. Quite often, wounded people assume God feels the same way about them—that they're useless, hopeless, and helpless. Their minds become filled with incorrect presumptions about God and about themselves.

We have the privilege of speaking God's truth into the lives of our children.

We have the privilege of speaking God's truth into the lives of our children. We don't have to be experts in theology to communicate life-changing biblical concepts. For instance, we can explain to our kids often and clearly:

• *"God designed you!"*

No matter the reasons for a child's birth, he or she is never a mistake or a "cosmic accident." God told Jeremiah (and us): "I knew you before I formed you in your mother's womb" (Jer. 1:5). King David wrote:

> You made all the delicate, inner parts of my body
>   and knit me together in my mother's womb.
> Thank you for making me so wonderfully complex!
>   Your workmanship is marvelous—how well I know it.

You watched me as I was being formed in utter seclusion, as I was woven together in the dark of the womb. (Ps. 139:13–15)

• *"You're God's masterpiece."*

God doesn't make junk! He beautifully and specifically crafts each person. In his letter to the Ephesians, Paul explained, "We are God's masterpiece. He has created us anew in Christ Jesus, so we can do the good things he planned for us long ago" (Eph. 2:10).

Like an artist who paints a beautiful portrait or landscape, God took His time to craft every part of us: eyes, nose, personality, gifts, and talents. God designed each of us individually and specifically.

You and your children are God's masterpieces. When we learn to see ourselves from His perspective, we will see how wonderful we really are. And when we believe this truth about ourselves, we will impart it to our children.

• *"God paid a high price for you!"*

Some kids see themselves as disposable, valueless, and not worth anyone's time and attention. How is the value of anything or anyone determined? By the price another is willing to pay for it. A baseball card is just a small piece of cardboard, but a 1909 Honus Wagner card recently sold for $2.8 million! The person who bought it believed it was quite valuable, but many moms throw out their kids' baseball cards because they think they're just clutter!

What's the value of a person? God put a price tag on human beings when He sent His Son to pay the ultimate price for us. Jesus died in our place, paid the debt we couldn't pay, and ransomed us from sin and hell to be adopted into God's family! In a letter to the Corinthians, Paul explained, "You do not belong to yourself, for God bought you with a high price" (1 Cor. 6:19–20). God was willing to pay a high price for us because He considers us and our children supremely valuable. We're worth more to Him than the stars in the sky! Our kids need to hear this message. So do we.

• *"God cares about the details of your life!"*

God didn't spin the universe into being and then leave us on our own. He's intimately involved in everything we do. God is omnipresent, which means He's with us (and with every atom in the universe) at every moment. And God is omniscient, which means He knows everything about . . . well . . . everything.

Jesus once told His followers, "What is the price of two sparrows—one copper coin? But not a single sparrow can fall to the ground without your Father knowing it. And the very hairs on your head are all numbered. So don't be afraid; you are more valuable to God than a whole flock of sparrows" (Matt. 10:29–31). You mean so much to God that He knows exactly how many hairs are on your head. When one falls out, He changes the number. Isn't that amazing?

If you want to help your children develop a healthy, positive self-concept, teach them to view themselves the way that God, their Master-Designer, sees them. They are His Masterpiece. He created them, and He cares about every detail of their lives.

> **If you want to help your children develop a healthy, positive self-concept, teach them to view themselves the way that God, their Master-Designer, sees them.**

2. Be intentional with your words.

Often, parents don't realize the power of their words. As we've seen, kids receive far too many negative messages from the media, their peers, and other adults. The last thing they need is for the people who love them unconditionally— their parents—to speak negative words to them.

Be careful with your words. Kids are sensitive and take your careless phrases to be the truth. Be honest, positive, and consistent. Kids can tell when parents are shading the truth or outright lying to them, so say what you mean and mean what you say. Often, out of anger, parents say things like, "Why can't you be more like your sister?" "Stop being such a baby!" "Don't you ever use your brain?" "You're the laziest person I know!" The parents may feel tremendous stress, and their words are cries of exasperation, but that's no excuse.

Some parents try to justify caustic messages to their children as attempts to be helpful. They insist, "They need a little correction now and then." Yes, children need correction, but loving, affirming correction—not the shattering, condemning kind.

Take a minute to look back over the last three days and take an inventory of all the messages you've given, spoken and unspoken, to your kids. The ratio should be at least five positive messages to each corrective one—and none of them should shame the child! Too often, parents react out of frustration and speak before they think. Solomon described the potential damage that can do: "The words of the reckless pierce like swords, but the tongue of the wise brings healing" (Prov. 12:18, NIV).

We must do more than restrain our negative messages. We need to make positive messages a normal part of our daily communication. Since Ashton and Jordan were little children, I've made a point to tell each of them three things each day. I grab them individually, hold them close, look them in the eye, and say, "I love you. I'm proud of you. I'm glad you're my daughter (or son)."

You might assume only little boys and girls need this degree of affirmation, but you would be wrong. Teenagers need this powerful, loving message because they're charting out a new identity and facing new challenges every day. When Jordan is a grown man and I'm old, he can expect me to call him at work and say, "Hey, son. I want you to know that I love you. I'm proud of you. I'm glad you are my son. . . . And could you stop by the store and bring me some adult diapers on your way home?"

I want my positive words to resonate in the minds of Ashton and Jordan. They may forget every other instruction, correction, or statement I make during the eighteen years they live in our home, but I want them to remember these three messages. In their darkest moments they'll remember, "Dad loves me. He's proud of me. He's glad I'm his child."

Come up with your own ways of affirming your love for your children. I have a friend who has a special statement he says to his children on Father's Day every year. When they call to wish him "Happy Father's Day," he tells them, "Because of you, every day is Father's Day for me." He told me, "Yeah, now that they're adults with kids of their own, they think it's kind of cheesy, but they know I mean it. I think they love to hear it every year."

Every word counts. Don't miss an opportunity to intentionally affirm your kids. Many days you may be the only one who is giving them positive messages. Your loving words go a long way to counteract all the negative messages your child receives all day long. Can you overdo it and seem insincere? Sure, but that's generally not the problem. As a rule of thumb, try to speak at least five positive, affirming, supportive, hopeful, loving messages for every correction—and *never* use shame, blame, or condemnation to control your kids.

3. Help your children discover their strengths.

Every child has been given a unique set of personality traits, skills, and abilities. As your children discover their talents, they will gain confidence and find ways to use them.

Most of us are wary of any kind of "performance review" at work because the focus tends to be more on the negatives than the positives—or maybe all we remember are the negatives even though much of what was said was positive. Parents can assume that their kids, especially teenagers, have the same predisposition to hear negative assessments. It's our job to convince them they're gifted and have a hope-filled future. We can help them celebrate their strengths!

In our part of the country (like every other part of America), sports is a big deal. My son, Jordan, tried playing football, basketball, and baseball, but he didn't excel at them. Like his dad, he's not a natural athlete. When he compared himself to other kids at his school, he got frustrated. More times than I can count, Cherith and I told him, "It's okay. The important thing is, you weren't afraid to try, and you gave it your all. Now let's try something else and discover what you do really well."

One year he decided to try out for the Christmas production at church. The director was amazed at Jordan's acting talent. In fact, Jordan got one of the lead roles in the production. He discovered that he has a genuine gift for acting and stage performance. He loved it!

But that's not his only talent. When Jordan was eight, he started tinkering with my computer. He used my video recorder to shoot videos of himself playing with his toys. Later he taught himself how to edit videos. Today Jordan has his own YouTube channel. He shoots and uploads videos for his subscribers. He even has a side business editing videos for his friends. He fancies himself a "mini media mogul." He discovered a true talent—for video production and for business.

Ashton has an amazing voice but was very shy when she was young. Cherith and I listened for hours as she sang around the house and lip-synced performances by her favorite artists. But unlike Jordan, Ashton would *never* perform publicly. When she was six, Ashton thought she wanted to come onstage with us at a Kids Camp and do the motions to the songs. As we started the first song, she took one look out at the crowd and burst into tears. She immediately ran offstage and solemnly vowed she would *never* go onstage again.

Cherith and I kept encouraging her. We wanted her to feel confident enough with her singing talent to share it with others, but she consistently refused. We didn't push too hard, and we continued to enjoy hearing her sing at our house.

One day Ashton told me she was going to try out for a solo in our Kids in Worship production, an event where the children of our church lead the adult congregation in worship. We were so proud of her for deciding to try out, but we were nervous that she would back out when she realized there would be nearly a thousand people in the audience. I don't know what happened in the mind and heart of that little girl, but she made it happen. She walked out there and nailed it! From that moment, we saw a major change in Ashton's self-esteem. She already knew she was a talented singer, and now she had the confidence to sing in public.

Soon after the production, Ashton tried out for the Youth Worship Team at church. She eventually was asked to be a part of the Worship Team leadership. Every week she's onstage in front of all of her peers, leading them in worship with tremendous confidence. When children discover their strengths, their self-esteem skyrockets.

To help your child discover his or her strengths, be creative, supportive, and patient. Here are some things Cherith and I have learned:

• *Encourage your child to try many different activities.*

Your children won't know if they're good at something if they never give it a shot. Too often, parents allow children to opt out of activities because they "just don't want to"—often before they even attempt it. A child can't know if she will enjoy an activity or be good at it if she never gives it a try.

But the other side of the equation is that there's no shame in trying and failing . . . or trying and not enjoying it. I'm not a bad person because I don't like hockey, and my kids aren't inferior in any way if Jordan doesn't enjoy playing baseball and Ashton isn't a math whiz. Trying a lot of different activities can be a good, healthy learning experience, but only if there's no pressure to excel at them all.

Trying a lot of different activities can be a good, healthy learning experience, but only if there's no pressure to excel at them all.

For instance, get your children involved in an art class, take them to the opera, encourage them to enter a short story competition, or sign them up for tee ball. Encourage them to try things that may not necessarily seem interesting at first. By expanding your children's horizons, you give them an opportunity to discover their strengths—and those strengths may be totally different from yours!

• *Ask questions to narrow the focus.*

As a follow-up to involvement in new activities, ask your kids open-ended questions about their experiences. Start by choosing three different activities that can be done at home—drawing, writing a story, building a playhouse, kicking a soccer ball, or any of dozens of other crafts and sports. Of those three, ask your child which one he prefers. As children get older, they have far more opportunities, and they need to learn to focus on the things they do best (and enjoy most).

One of the biggest problems for many adults is that they never find "the sweet spot" of their vocation. For instance, a person may be brilliant in a certain field and end up teaching the subject, yet he really doesn't like people! He would have done far better with a career in research or accounting in his chosen field.

We can help kids discern their "best fit" by asking "funneling questions" that help them uncover their true motivation, challenge, and desire. For instance, a young man was a gifted artist but was floundering in college. His father asked, "What do you see yourself doing in ten years?"

His son answered, "I'd like to be an artist."

"Why is that, son?"

"Because that's the one thing I have confidence in. It's the one thing I know I can do."

"What kind of art do you want to do?"

"I love painting and sculpting, but I need to make a living, so I'm thinking about graphic design."

His dad asked, "Don't you want to do what you really love?"

"I love to eat, Dad," his son laughed. "And besides, I'm thinking about going back to grad school in art after I establish myself."

"Wow, son. It looks like you're thinking this through really well."

"You know, Dad, I don't think it has been as clear as it is right now. Thanks for talking to me about it."

In an article for *The Parents League of New York*, Jenifer Fox observed, "To discover strengths, children must be prompted to funnel and narrow until they are able to precisely name the thing that most energizes them."[14]

• *Watch your child at play.*

You can often get a clear picture of your children's strengths by watching them play. Playtime is when their imagination runs wild and they're free to pursue their passions. As you watch, you'll learn a lot about their preferences and skills.

What activities bring your children joy? What keeps their attention for a long time? What is the one activity your child would choose over any other if given the choice? The answers to these questions will give you clues as to your child's strengths.

4. Show unconditional love.

Don't just show your love and approval when your kids perform well or when they tell you what you want to hear. One of the biggest opportunities you have to form your child's self-image is when your child fails or struggles.

Don't withhold love to punish and control your kids. Speak words of love *especially* when they are defiant. Affirm them *especially* when they mess up. Remind them that what they do—good or bad—never changes your love for them. Correct them, but do so in a spirit of grace, hope, and love. Correct the action; don't label the child.

The natural, human response to defiance and disobedience is to clamp down on our kids to control them or to run away to hide from the chaos. Neither of those reactions is loving and helpful. Children need to know that although you disapprove of the action they chose, your love for them is not determined by their performance.

> **Children need to know that although you disapprove of the action they chose, your love for them is not determined by their performance.**

Last summer Jordan spent the night with some friends. During the night, the boys got into a little mischief and ended up causing damage to some property. Jordan denied any involvement. Over and over and over he assured us that he was nowhere near the incident. We believed him.

Several months later Jordan confessed that he, indeed, had been involved. In fact, he was directly involved. It hurt us deeply that he had lied to us. We were angry, but we let our anger fuel a positive response.

Cherith and I discussed the consequences for Jordan's actions. We shared those consequences with him, but we added several important messages during our talk. We told him, "You lied to us, and you broke our trust. It was a bad decision, but you're so much more than this choice. This isn't you; you're not a liar. You're an honest young man who lied to get out of trouble. Learn from this. Be the honest, honorable person we know you to be. You can fix this!"

Cherith and I didn't deny his failure. We called it what it was: "You lied to us. You broke our trust." But we didn't let the lie become his identity; we didn't put a condemning label on him. In fact, we did the opposite. We affirmed what we believe to be true about him: "This isn't you; you're not a liar." It's important to speak words of affirmation especially during times of failure so you (and your child) can separate the action from the person.

That's what our heavenly Father does for us. When we fail, He forgives. He doesn't label us, remind us about it later, or hang it over our heads. It's over. It's done. Then He wraps His loving arms around us and shows us unconditional love. We were, are, and will always be His beloved children.

5. Model a healthy self-image for your child.

All day, every day you proclaim your self-concept to everyone around you, including your children. And make no mistake: your children are soaking in every word, action, attitude, raised eyebrow, and tone of voice. Make your self-directed messages positive ones. If you're excessively harsh on yourself, pessimistic, full of self-pity, or unrealistic about your abilities and limitations, your children will notice. They may become just like you, or they may respond in an opposite but equally destructive way. Either way, their lives will be shaped by your negativity.

Messages in regard to your own identity are just as important as the ones you communicate about your child's identity. How you interact with your child is important, but the child is also watching to see how you talk about yourself, treat yourself, and value yourself. For instance, if a mother is preoccupied with her looks—fat or slim, sloppy or elegant, old-fashioned or trendy—she shouldn't be surprised when her daughter begins to feel inadequate about her personal appearance. The message the mother sent the daughter for years was that physical appearance matters more than anything! The daughter heard the message loudly and clearly, whether the mother meant to send the message or not.

If you want to raise a child with strong self-esteem, nurture your own. Then your child will have a great role model to follow.

6. Avoid the comparison game.

We've identified the pitfalls of comparison, but the problem is inescapable. Your child is naturally going to compare himself or herself to others, so don't join in on that unhealthy activity. Don't compare your child's grades to those of a brother or sister. Don't say, "Why do you have to wear your hair like that? I wish you would dress like Chris." And by all means, don't compare your children to you when you were their age.

Comparison is a deadly game that's based on unfair rules. Kids develop at different rates. There are early developers, slow bloomers, and steady-as-you-go kids in every group, so comparing your child's results or performance can be completely unrealistic. Albert Einstein once said, "If you judge a fish by its ability to climb a tree, it will live its whole life believing that it is stupid."

Allow your children to be unique, develop at their own pace, and pursue the things that bring them—not just you— joy and satisfaction.

7. Be there for your child.

Be fully present. Show up. When your kids have a game, be their biggest cheerleader—but don't overdo it! When they have a school play, sit in the audience and clap for them. By showing up, you send the message, "You're important to me. I arranged my schedule to make sure that I could be here to see you do what you do best. I'm so proud of you, and I want to be there for the things that are important to you."

Maybe you aren't great with words. That's okay. Your presence speaks volumes to your kids. They know you're busy and have a thousand things pulling you in a thousand directions. They may not express their appreciation now, but be assured that you're speaking powerful messages to them by just showing up.

The failure to show up leaves an open wound. I have a good friend, Matt Taylor, who's a gifted, loving pastor. He told me, "For the majority of my life, and still to this day, my mom isn't very supportive of me. She never made it to any of my high school games, and she has never heard me preach in my six years of ministry. I've always wanted her to be involved. I understand that she's a single mom and was maxed out a lot of the time. I've never met my dad, and my mom always makes excuses about why she can't be there. It has caused me to question her love for me (as silly as it sounds). It seems that the only type of connection we have is simply out of her obligation. It hurts. She's the only family that I have, but her actions show that she really doesn't even care."

Being there speaks volumes to your kids.

No Matter What

Some of you reading this chapter may have cringed several times, and some of you may have cried. I'm not trying to heap blame on anyone. By reading this chapter, you've shown that you genuinely want to instill love, joy, and hope into the life of your child. I applaud that! We've looked at a lot of ways we can impart a healthy and positive self-concept to our children, but some of us need to start closer to home—in our own hearts and minds.

If *you* struggle with self-esteem, read this chapter again. Soak up the truths from God about His love for you. Believe that you're His masterpiece. Acknowledge the wounds you've been carrying for many years, and ask God to bring hope and healing. As He works deeply in you to shape a new sense of your God-given identity, you'll be able to speak words of love and life to your children.

There are three questions inherent in this chapter. We need to answer them, first for ourselves and then for our kids:

Who am I?

Whose am I?

Why am I here?

Bask in the love and grace of God. Soak up the forgiveness Jesus offers. Realize that you are more valuable to God than all the gold, diamonds, oil, and riches of the earth—even more treasured to God than the stars in the sky! And then communicate that wonder to your kids. It will make a difference.

Chapter 5

How to Talk to Your Kids About Making Wise Choices

Kids—all kids—make dumb decisions. Mistakes and poor choices are part of the process of learning and growing. When young people learn from their bad choices, they take steps toward a more meaningful, God-honoring life. However, failing to learn these lessons is a big problem. It's our job to help them gain wisdom in three different ways: vicariously, by watching others be wise or foolish; following God's way and obeying His directions; and suffering the consequences of dumb decisions. Unfortunately, too many of our lessons come from the last of the three!

We all want our kids to be wise. We train them, reason with them, encourage them, model for them, and do everything we can to impart godly wisdom and practical guidance. We spend eighteen years (sometimes more) monitoring their every move, correcting when necessary, and preparing for the day we'll set them free to go out into the world and make a life of their own.

We hope and pray that Solomon's proverb will be true of our children: "Direct your children onto the right path, and when they are older, they will not leave it" (Prov. 22:6).

No Guarantees

Hope and prayer, though, don't completely calm our fears. We instinctively ask, "How can I guarantee that my children will be wise and will walk with God? How can I be sure that all of the principles, lessons, and wisdom I've poured into them will actually stick when they launch out into the world?"

All of us have seen and heard horror stories of kids who grew up in godly homes, had amazing parents, and went to church every Sunday, but then left the nest and walked away from God into a lifestyle of sin.

The truth is there are no guarantees. I don't mean to be a pessimist, but it's true. As much as we want our children to choose to follow God's way that is set before them, they're individuals with their own wills. No matter how good and godly their parents may be, and no matter how committed they've been to children's church and youth groups, they make their own decisions in childhood, in adolescence, and after they leave home. Some parents want a three-step plan to assure their kids will always walk with God. There isn't one. But relax, there *are* clear principles to help us impart wisdom to our kids.

We live in a culture obsessed with getting ahead and assuring wins. We've developed little tolerance for failure or disappointment. If you can't guarantee the weight-loss program will help me drop twenty pounds, I'm not going to use it. If you can't guarantee I'll get a job on the first interview by using your training program, I'm not even giving it a try. We want guarantees on everything, and parenting is no different. We want a 100 percent money-back guarantee this will work and our kids will turn out great.

God, however, didn't give us a guaranteed plan; He gave us Himself, His grace, His truth, and His Spirit—and He gave each person the dignity and responsibility to make their own choices about Him and about every other aspect of life. We aren't robots; we're people created in God's image with the freedom to choose.

Ironically (but predictably), parents' aggressive attempts to guarantee that their kids will walk God's path often drive those kids away from God. It breaks the kids' hearts, the

parents' hearts, and God's heart. When parents microman-
age their children—spiritually, emotionally, relationally,
scholastically, and every other way—they rob their children
of two things: confidence and competence. Kids under this
kind of parenting soon believe they can't make their own
decisions, so they either blandly submit or defiantly rebel.
When they aren't allowed to think for themselves, or to try
and fail, they don't develop the skills it takes to make it in the
world. In trying to guarantee a child will love the Lord and
grow up to think exactly like them, the parents become the
biggest obstacle in their kid's development.

> **In trying to guarantee a child will love the
> Lord and grow up to think exactly like them,
> the parents become the biggest obstacle in
> their kid's development.**

The solution, of course, isn't a hands-off approach. The
extremes of being smothering or passive are equally destructive. There has to be another way, and there is.

My own children are still in the formative stage of adolescence, so I'm still learning how to be the parent they need
me to be. However, I've been a kids' pastor for twenty-two
years, and I've seen a lot of kids grow up. I've watched parents
use every conceivable technique to train their kids. Some of
these young people have grown into amazing leaders and

exemplary Christ followers, but some have fallen away and haven't returned to faith (not yet, anyway). I've learned the most by watching a few terrific parents help their kids become secure and confident young adults.

Even though there are no guarantees, parents and grandparents can implement some basic principles to train their children to make wise decisions that will draw them closer to God and help them become lifelong followers of Jesus Christ.

A Definition

Let's start by defining "wise decisions." Over the centuries, philosophers have defined and described wisdom in many different ways. Cultural differences, spiritual perspectives, and family backgrounds all shape our expectations of what it means to be wise.

What's wise to one may not seem wise to others. Not long ago, I participated in a 13.1-mile obstacle course race called the "Tough Mudder." Our team consisted of about twenty people who dove into freezing water, climbed over twenty-foot walls, and were shocked with 10,000 volts of electricity. Many people wouldn't consider that "wise." Of course, we loved it!

Since *wise decision* is a term that can be fairly subjective, let me define it for our purposes: Wise decisions are those that are in agreement with the Bible, directed by the Holy

Spirit, and promote the spiritual growth of individuals and the people they influence.

Obviously, not every decision your child makes will fall in line with that definition. Most kids won't consult the Bible when choosing what pair of shoes to wear. But there are plenty of issues—choosing friends, entertainment preferences, where they hang out, activities worth their time, how they use words, their purpose in life, and so on—that are important decisions that affect their future, their livelihood, and even their eternity. We want those decisions to be wise decisions. To combine two clichés: major on the majors, and don't sweat the small stuff.

Wisdom is a rare commodity in today's world. Raising kids who make wise decisions is a challenge in a society that continually promotes and glorifies unwise choices. In the generations before mass media, this pressure was restricted to their families and friends. Today's kids have the entire world at their fingertips. They can watch fools on YouTube and soak up images of the full range of unwise, destructive behaviors.

Practical Principles

It's tough to help children become wise, but it's not impossible. Cherith and I have learned some practical, helpful principles while raising our two children and watching other parents raise theirs.

If you want your child to make wise decisions:

Ask God for wisdom.

You can't impart wisdom to your child unless you first possess it. True wisdom doesn't come from experience, books, or training. True wisdom comes from God. James wrote, "If you need wisdom, ask our generous God, and he will give it to you. He will not rebuke you for asking" (James 1:5).

Our natural tendency, our default, is to assume that the way our parents raised us is the good, right, and godly way, and should be the model for how we raise our kids. Modeling is incredibly powerful, and the role model of our parents, for good or ill, has shaped all of us. The best parents, though, model dependence on God to acquire His insights and guidance. Don't simply try to pass on what your parents taught you. Family traditions may be helpful, but even more, you and your kids need godly wisdom. God is more than willing to give it if we'll just ask Him. Pray, and trust God to lead you as you impart His wisdom to your children.

Establish clear boundaries.

As your child grows from an infant to a toddler, boundaries are very specific and persistent, and they usually pertain to safety or appropriate social behavior. We spell it out for them: "Don't put the fork into the power outlet!" "You are not allowed to feed your lima beans to the cat!" Those days may seem exasperating, but at least the rules are pretty clear.

Things get more complicated when your child enters pre-school. As your child's world expands, the boundaries you set expand as well. You give more freedom for your child to make particular decisions—what shirt to wear, what games to play, and similar choices—but you have clear boundaries about getting ready for school, relating to siblings, homework, and the growing set of responsibilities around the house. For each of these, the child has a choice: follow, ignore, or defy. Boundaries are meaningless if there aren't clear and appropriate consequences, and the consequences need to be established *before* the problem happens!

> **At each stage of the child's development, setting boundaries and enforcing consequences are critical to forming a respectful, well-adjusted, mature person.**

When parents fail to enforce consequences, they send a message that the kids can get away with anything. That's a bad message when they're little children, and it's a dangerous message as they grow up. At each stage of the child's development, setting boundaries and enforcing consequences are critical to forming a respectful, well-adjusted, mature person.

We need to communicate—clearly and often—that the boundaries we set aren't for our comfort and convenience; they are steppingstones to help the child learn, grow, and excel in life. We set boundaries and enforce them because we love our kids.

Explain the "why."

Don't just tell your kids the "what." Also explain the "why." If you don't explain your reasons for a decision, you can be sure they'll ask. Take a look at the pattern of your responses. "Because I said so" isn't a helpful explanation! If that's your normal response to your child's questions, dig a little deeper. You might get tired of explaining the rationale behind every decision to your kids, but that's the way they learn how to make wise decisions.

You're not programming a computer. Your kids don't have motherboard brains. You can't just fill them full of "if-then," "cause-effect" equations and expect them to make wise decisions. Talk to them about *why* one choice is better than another one.

Of course, their obedience isn't predicated on their complete understanding of an issue. For instance, a young child may want to eat a candy bar just before dinner, and you say, "No, that will spoil your dinner." The child may pitch a fit. If you try to explain the physiological workings of sugar on the brain at that point, your child will cry louder (and think you're nuts). There are times, especially when children are little, that explanations don't work very well. For those instances, our best explanation is at a higher plane: We look the child in the eye and tell him, "I know what's best for you, and you need to trust me." As kids grow up, however, they usually need more specific explanations.

Practice what you preach.

Too many parents communicate the harmful message: "Do as I say, not as I do." They tell their kids to be respectful, but their children hear them gossip and say horrible things about a friend. They tell their kids to stay calm, but they explode in anger when things don't go the way they planned. They tell their kids to pray, but they fret about every little problem. An honest self-analysis can be painful, but it's necessary if we're going to be the parents God wants us to be.

Children learn more by watching you than by listening to you. What example are you setting? What do they see in the good times, in the bad times, when you're under stress, and when others are rude to you? If your kids aren't doing what you tell them to do, consider the harsh possibility that what you do shouts so loudly they can't hear what you're saying to them.

Kids who watch parents make wise choices become equipped to make their own wise choices. In my experience of watching kids, the pattern is very clear: foolish parents raise foolish kids, disobedient parents raise disobedient kids, driven parents raise driven kids, optimistic parents raise optimistic kids, and loving parents raise loving kids.

We can talk to our kids about the importance of going to church and being taught God's Word, but then do they see us skip church at the smallest inconvenience? We can try to convince them that they need to pray, but do they see us praying alone and hear us pray for the family? We can instruct them to tell the truth, but do they see us exaggerate, use half-truths, or tell outright lies? Kids emulate their parents. We can't lead our children down a path that we aren't walking.

> ## We can't lead our children down a path that we aren't walking.

Connect children's decisions to God's Word.

Many people complain that the Bible isn't clear enough to give us direction for our lives, but in many cases the people who voice this complaint haven't read it! Actually, the Bible is crystal clear about a wide range of extremely important issues, and it provides wisdom to help us make decisions about things that aren't specifically spelled out. For instance, God's Word gives clear instructions to our children about:

- What kind of friends should they choose?

- Should they get drunk?

- Should they obey their parents?

- Should they cheat on this test?

- Should they lie to get out of trouble?

- Should they have sex before they're married?

- Should they pray, give, serve, study God's Word, and trust God for wisdom?

For other decisions, Scripture gives general guidelines to help people discern God's will. For instance, the Bible doesn't tell us which movies to watch, but it tells us to guard our minds. It doesn't tell us what job to pursue, but it reminds us that God has given us talents and will give us opportunities to use them. It doesn't specify which shirt or shoes we should buy. All of our purchases, though, can be shaped by the principles of stewardship and generosity. In other words, if I spend $200 on a pair of shoes, I won't have as much to give to help those who have no shoes at all, and I won't have as much saved for a more important purchase.

So there's no subject for which the Bible doesn't provide either clear directions or general principles to guide our choices. In conversation around the dinner table, on the field, in the car, and before bedtime, make the connection between the Word of God and the challenges your kids face. God's Word is infallible; it's perfect, without error. Your children can argue with your opinion, but God's Word is clear and powerful.

Paul wrote Timothy, "All Scripture is inspired by God and is useful to teach us what is true and to make us realize what is wrong in our lives. It corrects us when we are wrong and teaches us to do what is right. God uses it to prepare and equip his people to do every good work" (2 Tim. 3:16–17).

Walk your child through the decision-making process.

When children are very young, they're usually with you enough so that you can help them think things through as they make decisions. As they get older, we often have to carve out time to have meaningful conversations with them. Talking your children through the process *before* the choice is a lot easier than helping them repair a mistake later!

Here are some questions to ask. Some are more appropriate for older kids, but you can adapt them for younger ones.

- What does the Bible say about your situation and your choices?

- What are you asking God to do for you in this situation?

- Do you have peace about this decision? Why or why not?

- How will this choice affect our family and those you care about?

- Are you trying to get as close as you can to sin without technically sinning? How can you tell?

- Will this choice make it harder or easier to share your faith with others?

- What does your pastor or spiritual leader suggest you do?

Even if you ask great questions, kids will still make some dumb choices. In most cases, that's no big deal—unless you make it a really big deal! Instead of overreacting in fear or blame, you can turn the responsibility back to the child and ask, "What are you going to do about it now?" Kids will learn far more from a little trial and error than if you make every decision for them. Having good problem-solving and decision-making skills will help your children learn to be wise, strong, and mature when they leave home and become adults.

As your children grow, allow them to make more decisions for themselves.

When your children move into adolescence, you should gradually stop *telling* them what to do and increasingly *ask* them, "What do *you* think you should do?" Allow *them* to make the decisions, and then—unless it would clearly break God's law or civil law—allow them to experience the consequences of their decisions. Don't protect them and don't correct them. Increasingly, treat them like the adults they are becoming.

Too often, parents are in "fix it" mode and try to solve problems for their children—even before a problem occurs. Rather than making a decision for your children, help them make it themselves. Then . . .

Don't shield your child from consequences.

Parents often tell me they're terribly afraid their children will fail in life. Watching your kids fail makes you feel helpless, angry, and sad. You worry about everything from their self-esteem and social development to their future success. Often, parents are even more worried about their own reputations as great parents!

Some parents try to teach their children a lesson without allowing them to experience the pain of the consequences of their failure. That's a problem . . . a huge problem. When children aren't allowed to live with the results of a bad decision, even if painful, they rarely learn important lessons.

I know this is difficult for many parents because I've been there. Some time ago, Jordan made a mistake that turned out to be expensive—about $1,000. I could have lectured him long and hard, paid the bill, and hoped he learned the lesson, but I knew that's not how young people learn. He needed to feel the pain of his mistake. I swallowed hard and told him the cost was his responsibility. To pay it, he cleaned out his savings and all the money he had made by working that summer.

Was that an easy path for me to take with him? Not at all. I'll always remember the look on his face when he handed me his life's savings, but it was worth it. He learned something that day he'll never forget. He may have been upset with me for a little while, but not for long. We later had some wonderful conversations about the experience. I got to explain why I wanted him to take responsibility for his actions, and I told him it would make him a better man—and it has.

For a variety of reasons, many parents don't want their kids to feel uncomfortable about anything, even when they know it's beneficial for the child to pay a price for his choices. Some parents will fight the school, fight with other parents, and fight with their spouse—all in the vain effort to keep the child from feeling uncomfortable. They genuinely believe their compulsion to protect is best for the child, but they're stunting the child's development.

In our culture, protecting your child from discomfort—and the pain of any conceivable disappointment—has become associated with effective parenting. That's a false assumption and a dangerous path for the whole family. Yet in many circles, and especially Christian circles, if your child suffers at all from the normal pain of growing up, you're considered a bad parent.

I'm not suggesting that you should seek opportunities to make your child feel miserable, but if a child suffers the natural consequence of unwise decisions, you shouldn't interfere. Don't "rescue" your child from the pain of bad choices.

Don't "rescue" your child from the pain of bad choices.

Many parents need a radical reorientation. They need to see that when children feel disappointed, frustrated, angry, or sad, they are in an ideal position to gain wisdom and develop important coping skills. The first thing they learn is to avoid similar situations. So if your child is called on in class to answer a homework question but didn't do his assignment, he can learn to avoid the embarrassment by doing his homework—not by having his mother tell the teacher not to call on him anymore because it makes him feel bad.

When you shield your child from consequences, he starts to think he should never have to feel anything unpleasant in life. This quickly develops into a false sense of entitlement. He learns that he doesn't really have to be prepared in school because his parents will complain to the teacher, who will stop calling on him or expecting his homework to be in on time. The teacher will expect less from him because of his parents' intervention. He learns to confront a problem by letting his parents "power up" rather than developing the crucial character trait of responsibility. This approach gives the child (and the parent) immediate relief, but it robs the child of confidence and competence.

Don't shield your children from the consequences of their sin. Allow them to feel the pain and grow from it. Then . . .

Evaluate the decision with your child.

Talking to a child about the results of a choice doesn't have to feel like a business meeting. It can be relaxed, supportive, and honest. Don't accuse, and don't assume the worst. Simply ask, "How do you think that went?" The child's perception may be very different from yours—maybe more pessimistic, or maybe more optimistic. You don't need to correct much, if at all. Especially value the perceptions of older kids.

When you evaluate an unwise decision with your child, here are three important questions to ask:

• *"What part did you play in this problem?"*

This question usually leads to a crucial insight: Your child can't change other people's behavior and decisions, only his or her own. And again, avoid blaming or condemning. Too often, an exasperated parent blurts out, "You're so stupid!" A better response might be a question: "How was that unwise?"

When asked what part he played in a bad decision, a child might respond, "I don't know."

You can respond by saying, "Well, let's think about it. Where did you get off track?" "Where did things go wrong for you?" or "When did you first realize you were in trouble?"

If your child still can't identify the point when things went wrong, you can offer a suggestion or two. For instance, if the child didn't do his homework, you might say, "It seems to me you got off track when you didn't have your homework ready when your teacher called on you. The part you played was not being prepared."

- *"What are you going to do differently next time?"*

In any analysis and conversation about a problem, a parent can then ask, "What would you do differently if you could do it over?" This question often generates rich conversation, but remember to listen far more than you talk. Give your child positive feedback and tell her that you're proud she took on this challenge.

At every point and whenever possible, let your children come up with their own solutions instead of providing the answer for them.

For the child who didn't do his homework, a parent might ask, "What are you going to do differently the next time you have a homework assignment?" Or, "What are you going to do differently next time so that if your teacher calls on you, you won't get embarrassed?" Or, "What are you going to do differently next time to pass the test?" This is a big question in this conversation with your child, because it gets him to see other, healthier ways of responding to the problem.

At every point and whenever possible, let your children come up with their own solutions instead of providing the answer for them. Value their intelligence, autonomy, and responsibility. If their failure is a threat to you, that's your problem, not theirs. As your children grow up, do more coaching than smothering. If you sense resistance or defiance, stop and ask, "What's going on right now? You seem upset with me." Don't overreact. Invite honest dialogue.

The problem may be that your child feels condemned. If that's the case, offer reassurance and separate the temporary bad performance from your permanent strong acceptance. Your child may agree with you, he may try to defend himself, or he may feel ashamed. Again, assure him that the situation will build character and wisdom. If the child tries to dodge responsibility, come back to the initial question, "What part did you play?"

If resistance continues, you may need to point out, "It seems to me like you're making an excuse for not having your homework done." Or, "I feel like you're blaming me for not making sure you did your homework." Or, "Are you blaming your teacher for not having your homework done?" The possibilities are endless. The point is to have an open and honest dialogue with your child so he accepts responsibility for his part in the problem.

• *"What did you learn from this?"*

This question completes the loop of gaining wisdom from analyzing a problem. In the case of the child who didn't do his homework, a parent might ask, "What did you learn from being embarrassed when your teacher called on you?" Or, "What did you learn from not passing the test?" The child's ability to formulate and verbalize the lesson helps him internalize it, remember it, and apply it next time.

These are important questions to ask when evaluating a child's unwise decision, but we need to be realistic. Children are going to fail. They're going to be disappointed in themselves, and we're going to be disappointed in their poor choices. When that happens ...

Pick them up, dust them off, and let them make another decision.

A few bad decisions might be cataclysmic, but most don't fall in that abysmal category. Some parents overreact to virtually any failure by their children. They tell their spouse, their friends, and maybe even the child: "That was horrendous! Nothing will ever be the same! Trust is shattered! The future is ruined!" That's not exactly the most gracious, affirming, and hopeful statement a parent can make. It's much better to say, "Yes, it was a mistake, but you'll do better next time. You've learned an important lesson. Now try it again."

All people on the planet perform better when others are supportive of them. Your kids will bounce back if they're convinced you still believe in them—especially after they've blown it. Trusting them to make a better decision next time is the best medicine you can give. It empowers them, shows confidence in them, and gives them freedom to try again.

A Learning Curve . . . for Us

As you've read those ten principles, you probably conducted a silent self-assessment. How did you do? In which areas are you doing pretty well, and which ones need some improvement? Learning to acquire wisdom isn't just for our kids; we need more of God's wisdom to be the best parents we can be. Some of us have been too passive, and some have been too controlling and demanding of our kids. Our children face a steep learning curve as they grow into mature young adults, and we face similar challenges as we trust God for wisdom to parent them.

The goal of parenting isn't making sure our kids never fail; it's instilling wisdom and confidence so they have the courage to try new things, experience the joy of succeeding and growing, and develop the ability to learn from their mistakes.

Be your children's biggest fan. Be a parent who trusts them, teaches them, and walks them through the process of making wise decisions so that when they are on their own, they can thrive.

The points in this chapter aren't simply academic. Some of us have children who have made very bad decisions, causing the whole family to suffer. Relationships are strained, and a wall of defiance or shame prevents the give and take of love. Other children appear aimless and unmotivated, or defiant and rebellious. We've tried to help them, but they turn away in disgust. Should we give up on them? No way.

Jesus gave us an example of what to do in these situations. The parable of the prodigal son (Luke 15:11–32) shows us a father who had done everything to train up his son in the way he should go, but his younger son still foolishly left home and squandered his entire life savings. The dad didn't give up on him. He allowed his son to experience the consequences of his sin—all the way to the pigpen—but he never stopped praying and waiting for his son to return.

As we pray and watch, maybe, just maybe, our kids will "come to their senses" and return home. When they do, what will they find? The father in Jesus' story didn't stand with his arms folded, waiting for his son to grovel at his feet, and he didn't remind his son of his stupid decisions. He forgave him and welcomed him with open arms. The father loved the son even before he repented, and the son's repentance restored a strained relationship. The father's love never wavered.

It's never too late to become the parents God wants us to be. We can practice good decision making, and we can ask God to work in our children's lives. We can train them in the way of righteousness. We can allow them to make their own decisions, and when they fail, let them experience the consequences of those bad decisions. But of course, we never stop loving and praying for them.

My hope for you—and for your kids and grandkids—is that God will give you the supernatural ability to make wise decisions that are in agreement with the Bible, directed by the Holy Spirit, and promote the spiritual growth of individuals and the people they influence.

Chapter 6

How to Talk to Your Kids About Divorce

It was a normal Sunday afternoon in 1998. I was twenty-five years old, newly married, and serving fulltime as a children's pastor at a church in Dallas, Texas. I was also the worship leader for the evening services, and that afternoon I was preparing for our rehearsal.

Suddenly my pager (remember those?) buzzed. I looked down to see my parents' phone number on the display. I assumed they needed something. I walked down to my office to give them a call. (No cell phones back then.)

The moment they answered, I could tell something was wrong. Both of them were on the phone. My father said solemnly, "Brian, would you mind holding for a second while we get Karen (my sister) on three-way calling?"

I said, "Sure," but I was already feeling apprehensive. A few moments later, my sister joined the conversation.

Without any introductory small talk, my parents began one of the toughest conversations they ever dreamed of having with their children. They informed my sister and me that after twenty-nine years of marriage, they were getting a divorce. They handled the conversation as delicately as they could, but Karen and I were stunned and devastated. After they hung up, I just sat in my office in total shock and feeling crushed. I knew my parents were struggling, but I never dreamed things would come to this point.

I went back to the worship rehearsal and tried to act like nothing had happened. I attempted to speak to the worship team, but I was mute. When I realized I couldn't continue, I asked them to give me a minute and walked down to my pastor's office. As I opened the door, he was sitting at his desk. I slowly closed the door, turned around, and opened my mouth to explain what had happened, but again, no words came out. I began to sob like a baby.

Pastor Wilson prayed with me, and then he walked me out to my car and sent me home to be with Cherith. I cried for hours. I think it scared Cherith half to death. She had never seen me so broken.

It doesn't matter how old you are or where you are in life, the news of your parents' divorce always hits you like a ton of bricks.

Broken Dreams

As I've worked with children for over twenty years, I've repeatedly seen how news of their parents' divorce shatters their world. I wasn't ready to deal with it as an adult, and I'm sure it's even more difficult for a child to process this world-changing information. Everything they know, everything they depend on for emotional stability, is lost in an instant. They may have detected major issues in the parents' relationship for years, or perhaps one parent was suddenly shocked to discover a history of infidelity for the other. Whether the decision to divorce is immediate or drawn out, it devastates everyone involved. Quite often the parents are so traumatized they don't know how to help their children cope. It's always a tragedy, no matter how amicably the split happens.

Divorce is a difficult issue to discuss with children, especially with younger children who have no way to comprehend the complex and emotionally charged factors involved. Many parents are already distraught about the shattered dreams of a happy marriage, so they find it hard to talk to their kids about it. Some share far too much and become dependent on the children for emotional stability, which puts kids in a very awkward position. Others "go dark" and don't talk at all about the most traumatic event in the history of their family.

A close friend of mine, Twyla, told me, "One morning when I was seven years old, I woke up and my dad was gone.

He didn't explain why he left, and neither did my mom. I had no idea what was going on. I was confused and hurt. I cried every day for a long time. One day my second grade teacher called my mom to tell her how much I was hurting. My parents didn't handle their divorce with honesty and compassion. It would have been hard enough if they had explained things to me, but their silence deeply confused me and left me feeling hurt and angry . . . at them, at myself, and at God."

Some parents are willing to have an initial discussion to inform their children about their decision to divorce, but they rarely approach the subject again. One conversation isn't enough. When children aren't encouraged (or even allowed) to process their confusion and anxiety, hurts multiply as they live with the poisonous effects of their parents' unresolved suffering and resentment, combined with their own pain, fear, and anger.

Divorce is only one variable in the complex relationships of single-parent homes, divorce, and remarriage. The principles in this chapter are focused on the children of parents who are in the process or have already divorced, but they can be adapted and applied to single parents who have never married or broadened to apply to kids in blended families.

A recent study shows that in the broader American culture, 43 percent of marriages end in divorce, and depending on the state, between 26 and 47 percent of children live in single-parent homes.[15] More than 2,000 blended families are formed every day, but more than two-thirds of those fail within six years.[16]

I'm not writing about the sanctity of marriage, and I'm not offering advice to couples who are struggling. I'm not a marriage counselor, although I recognize the importance of this topic. In fact, the concepts in this chapter are important for *all parents* because virtually every child has friends from households that are currently experiencing a breakup or have gone through a divorce and are living with the consequences.

The Negative Effects of Divorce

By studying God's Word, we can all agree that divorce is never God's plan. I don't think it's ever anyone's plan. Nobody gets married thinking, "I sure can't wait to divorce this person one day." God's desire is that marriages thrive and last "until death do us part." Unfortunately, divorce happens. When it does, it affects everyone involved. Often, it disproportionately affects the children in an extremely negative way.

I've seen the devastation of divorce in the faces of parents and their kids. Confusion, resentment, discouragement, and depression are common results. If those emotions aren't resolved with love, honesty, and time, it deeply affects future relationships. Hurt people hurt people, and they often don't even know why they have difficulties in relationships. In the lives of children, a few of the most common results of divorce include:

Increased stress

No matter what age children are when their parents announce the breakup of their home, kids are never emotionally prepared for the shock. Stress shows up in many different ways. Relationally, kids may become defiant, or they may withdraw. Emotionally, they may become hardened and defiant, or they may regularly burst into tears. Physically, the stress often finds the weakest part of the person's body; headaches, stomachaches, and other gastrointestinal problems are common. Even the most mundane, everyday decisions can become difficult.

> No matter what age children are when their parents announce the breakup of their home, kids are never emotionally prepared for the shock.

Lack of stability

When parents split up, the most secure point in the child's universe is shaken and destroyed. God has made us to be relational beings, and the home is the first and foremost place of rest, comfort, and security. When that's disrupted, the child naturally questions the validity and reliability of everything and everyone. In addition, the child is suddenly forced to move back and forth from mom's house to dad's house, finding it difficult to ever feel settled and often feeling like a pawn in their blame game.

Eroded or shattered trust

When their security crumbles, children may put up walls and refuse to trust anyone, even those who are the most stable, loving people in their lives. Or in contrast, they may trust too much, putting their faith in untrustworthy people in the hope that trusting someone will make them feel safe again.

Irresponsibility or hyper-responsibility

Everything the kids have known has been turned upside down. The parents have been trying to teach their kids to be responsible, but now the children wonder, *What's the use?* They may neglect homework, cleaning their rooms, taking showers, and doing the normal things they've been doing for years. Or they may react in the opposite way, trying to earn their parents' love by being overly responsible. Some kids use their exemplary behavior as a bargaining chip in an attempt to get their parents to reconcile. It's magical thinking, but it shows the desperation of the child to restore a happy home.

Grandparents and other extended family members can provide much-needed stability and support during the confusing and painful time before, during, and after the divorce, but be careful. Some extended family members become furious at "that man" or "that woman" for hurting their beloved son or daughter, sister or brother. Extended family members may be a great source of wisdom, insight, and hope, or they can throw more gasoline on the fire of resentment!

How to Talk to Your Child if You Are Getting a Divorce

For years we thought the divorce rate in the church was about the same as the broader American society—around 50 percent. But recent research shows a different picture. In *The Good News About Marriage*, Harvard-trained analyst Shaunti Feldhahn reports that among couples who value their faith, the divorce rate is between 15 and 20 percent.[17] This shows that a vibrant relationship with God really matters!

When people think the divorce rate includes half of those who get married, they may feel that it's inevitable—or at least understandable—that their marriage would break up. But that's not the case! If both spouses are willing to take steps of faith, most marriages can be saved.

So I really wish this part of the chapter weren't necessary, but it is. If you're thinking about ending your marriage, let me encourage you to take these steps in communicating with your kids:

1. Wait until the decision is final.

Don't include your children in discussions of a *possible* divorce. Kids don't need to be overwhelmed by the emotional rollercoaster of "we are" and then "no, we aren't" getting a divorce. Never mention divorce to a child until it's an absolute certainty.

Some parents feel uncomfortable with this advice. The breakup, or the possibility of it, has been on the back burner of their minds for months or even years, and it eventually begins to consume every waking moment. They want to be honest with their kids, and to be truthful, they would like some support from them during such a hard time. However, this is a time when parents need to think more about the child than themselves. Even though they may feel as if they're "hiding something," it's very confusing for a child to hear, "Mom and Dad are thinking about getting a divorce." This announcement creates unnecessary anxiety and stress for the child.

2. Tell the child as a couple.

Unless one of the parents is violent, in jail, or has abandoned the family—which are devastating circumstances, but rare—it's best for both parents to talk to the child at the same time. This allows both parents to take some responsibility, lessens the pressure on the child to take sides, and minimizes confusion. The child hears the story only once instead of getting multiple (possibly contrasting) versions of the story. By telling the child together, parents also communicate that it was a mutual decision, which helps the child to avoid blaming one parent, which is very common and very destructive. There's a more important reason, too: It helps preserve your child's sense of trust in both parents.

3. Avoid details.

Your child doesn't need to hear the long, sad, and perhaps sordid story of the dissolution of the marriage. Simply explain that you, as a couple, have been having problems in your relationship, sought counseling in an attempt to resolve the problems, but have now decided that the best thing is to get divorced.

> **Your child doesn't need to hear the long, sad, and perhaps sordid story of the dissolution of the marriage.**

Even if there has been an affair, financial misconduct, or a criminal offense, the child should not have to hear all the unpleasant details. Older children will quickly pick up on plenty of cues from the relational tension in the home, and they may ask a lot of questions before the final decision is made. Invite the child to ask questions, but give answers that are limited and appropriate for the age of the child. Don't provide details that will only confuse them.

In addition, don't include children in discussions about the necessary legal or financial details regarding the divorce. Divorces are ugly. Children will have a hard enough time just dealing with the separation of their parents. They don't need to be forced to deal with more complex issues as well.

4. Tell the truth.

Don't give too many details, but by all means, be honest. Some parents want to protect their children by whitewashing the situation. Linda Ranson Jacobs of Divorce Care For Kids writes, "Answer with truthfulness and honesty on the child's developmental level and understanding. Never lie to a child."[18] That means never! A child may ask, "Mom, I know Dad has a girlfriend. What do you think about that?" The mom can respond, "You know, that's a question you need to ask your dad."

It's easy to lie. In the heat of the moment, parents are tempted to dodge the truth and say anything that promises to immediately resolve the tension. One child overheard that her dad had an affair and asked her mother about it, but the mother quickly answered, "No, he wasn't having an affair. None of that happened." But it did happen, and the child knew it. She felt betrayed twice—from one parent's infidelity and the other's lies.

Being honest isn't easy when you don't have all the answers and the kids are feeling scared or guilty about the breakup. Be wise about how much you tell them, but always tell them whatever they need to know at that moment.

5. Avoid the blame game.

No matter how angry you may be at your spouse, and no matter how justified you feel at pointing your finger, don't pin all the blame for the divorce on your spouse. Blaming your spouse immediately puts the children squarely in the middle, and they're forced to decide whose side they'll be on. In a relational triangle, two people take sides against the third one, they keep secrets, and they manipulate to win at all costs. Avoid triangles! They're not healthy for anyone involved.

6. Assure your child it's not his or her fault.

Children instinctively blame themselves for the breakup, even if they don't voice their responsibility (younger ones especially, but often older children as well). People have an innate sense of justice, and with it, an innate sense that someone must be blamed. When children aren't mature enough to assign responsibility appropriately, they tend to take it on themselves. Their thinking may seem almost comical, but it's tragic. For instance, a girl may assume her parents are getting divorced because she's not pretty enough, or a boy may conclude his parents are splitting up because he didn't clean his room or do well enough in school. The fact that there's no connection between these factors and the parents' decision doesn't matter—the child *assumes* a connection. After the decision is announced, the child may believe that changes in behavior or performance will somehow bring the parents back together.

Tell your children in clear terms that divorce is an adult decision and has nothing to do with them. Isolina Ricci, a psychotherapist and author of *Mom's House, Dad's House for Kids*, offers a suggestion of how to word the explanation: "Sometimes things happen with mommies and daddies. We're really sorry that it happened, but it's not anything you've done."[19]

Tell your children in clear terms that divorce is an adult decision and has nothing to do with them.

7. *Give the child a clear plan.*

Whether your kids express fear, worry, or relief about your separation and divorce, they will want to know how their own day-to-day lives might change. Be prepared to answer these and plenty of other questions:

- Who will I live with?

- Where will I go to school?

- Will I move?

- Where will each parent live?

- Where will I go to church?

- Where will we spend holidays such as Thanksgiving and Christmas?
- Will I still get to see my friends?
- Can I still go to camp this summer?
- Can I still do my favorite activities?

When you explain the plan, be as clear and detailed as possible. A mother might say, "You're going to live with me during the week. I'll take you to school and pick you up as usual. Your dad will come over to pick you up every Thursday night so you can be together. And every other weekend, you'll stay at your dad's new house."

Kids need to know what happens next. Have the details already worked out with your spouse (or ex) so you can present a united front to the child when you have the conversation.

8. Give an assurance: "We'll be okay."

Divorce is hard. Undoubtedly and inescapably, every person involved suffers pain. They will be angry, deeply hurt, confused, and fearful about the future. Each person has to face uncertainty and change. Through all of it, your child needs a bedrock of assurance that the pain isn't all there is or will be in life. There's hope for a better future.

Children naturally feel insecure after a divorce. A friend of Linda Ranson Jacobs shares her story of how instability can last a long time:

My mom and dad got a divorce when I was in third grade. I knew there were some problems, and one day my dad came home and he said, "Your mom and I are getting a divorce," and I followed him upstairs, and he packed a suitcase. I stood in the window, and I watched him as he walked down the sidewalk while he carried the suitcase. And the only thing I could think about was my safety was inside that suitcase. As an adult, I still don't feel safe today.[20]

9. Set up the next conversation.

The initial talk about the divorce is important, but children aren't likely to process all of their emotions and thoughts in a single conversation. It's unreasonable to expect them to be able to think clearly when their world has just been rocked. At the conclusion of the first talk, let the child know that in a few days you will talk again and answer any questions.

It's not enough just to leave the door open by saying, "Come to me whenever you want to talk about the divorce." Take the initiative and set up the next conversation. Tell the child, "I know you have a lot of questions, and you have a lot of powerful emotions, too. In a few days, I want us to talk again. Nothing is off limits. I want you to know that I love you, I'm here for you, and we'll all work through this together."

10. Pray with your child.

Remind your child that God is greater than any problem you face, including divorce. Explain that God can help all of you through the emotions and pain of divorce. He can provide the comfort and peace you all need in the midst of instability and insecurity.

Don't just talk *about* God; talk *to* Him. Pray with your child, asking God to help each person heal from the emotional wounds. Pray that God will help each person choose forgiveness instead of bitterness, love instead of resentment, and wisdom for the road ahead.

After a Divorce

Some of the most important decisions you'll make—and the most important conversations you'll have with your child—will come after the divorce is final. It often takes six to eight months before the full impact of the divorce hits the children. As those months pass, each holiday brings up many memories of the past, powerful emotions in the present, and concerns about the future—for everyone involved. Anticipate the ups and downs of the process of grieving and healing, and engage your child in loving, supportive, honest conversations.

Here are some things to keep in mind as you have ongoing conversations with your child after the divorce:

Anticipate the ups and downs of the process of grieving and healing, and engage your child in loving, supportive, honest conversations.

1. Stay emotionally engaged with your child.

Some kids try to please their parents by acting as if everything is fine, or they try to avoid painful feelings by denying that they feel any anger or sadness. However, signs of unrelieved stress come out eventually—at school, or with friends, or in changes to their appetite, behavior, or sleep patterns.

With their parent's divorce, children go through a process similar to grieving the death of a loved one. In essence, they're grieving the death of their parents' marriage and their own sense of security and happiness. Grieving is always messy, so provide a lot of support and understanding, and allow your children plenty of time to work through it. During the process, encourage them to express their emotions openly and honestly—especially the painful ones that may make you feel uncomfortable. Assure them that you value their feelings and you take their emotions seriously.

2. Help your child find the words.

Sometimes children act out in anger because they don't know how to express sadness or grief. Help your child find the words to express the full range of emotions. You might say, "It seems as if you're angry right now." As the conversation continues, you might ask, "Do you know what's making you feel so angry?" Some children (and adults) are more in touch with one emotion than another. For instance, a child might be able to express his anger, but he may not be able to identify the fear that triggers his anger and makes him feel out of control. She may be aware of her fear of being abandoned, but she may not feel safe enough to express anger at the ones who seem to have left her behind.

Be a good listener. Sometimes your child may say things that are hard for you to hear. Listen anyway—and listen without reacting. Legitimize children's feelings and help them process their emotions.

Be sensitive, be wise, and look beneath the surface, but don't push too hard to uncover buried emotions. If the child becomes depressed, seek professional help with a competent physician or counselor. Gently, patiently, and persistently guide your children through their emotions, helping them find the words for their feelings.

3. Offer unqualified support.

From time to time (but not so often that it becomes weird) put your arm around your child and ask, "Is there anything I can do to help you feel better?" Your son or daughter may just shrug and say, "I don't know," so you might suggest taking a walk together, going to the zoo, praying together, or holding a favorite stuffed animal.

Play can be very therapeutic for a small child dealing with loss. Many children act out their emotions and perceptions in drawing or in play. A sand pile, colored pens and paper, finger-paints, or bathtub toys provide a pallet for them to express what's going on inside them.

4. Invest in your own emotional, spiritual, physical, and relational health.

Parents are often so concerned with their children they ignore their own health during the months before and following the divorce. Separation and divorce are highly stressful, and the addition of custody issues and financial pressures are a recipe for burnout.

Each parent needs to find ways to manage stress in order to be loving, wise, and strong for the children. A prescription for all of us all the time, but especially for those under stress, includes exercise, eating healthy foods, and getting plenty of sleep. If you take care of your own health, you'll be strong for your kids.

5. Forgive.

No matter what circumstances led to the divorce, there will be deep wounds. If we aren't careful, bitterness can become more real than the grace of God. Hurt people have a natural tendency to replay upsetting conversations in their minds, relive painful events, recall insults, and blame the spouse for all past, present, and future pain. Don't give in to this temptation. It will ruin you.

"But Brian, you don't understand the depth of my pain. It just doesn't seem possible for me to fully forgive my ex." You're right. On your own, you can't forgive. Yet be aware that we don't forgive out of a vacuum. We have a resource that gives us the power and motivation to forgive those who have hurt us. Bitterness can only be overcome by a deep, life-changing experience of the forgiveness God has provided for our own sins. Paul explains in his letter to the Ephesians: "Get rid of all bitterness, rage, anger, harsh words, and slander, as well as all types of evil behavior. Instead, be kind to each other, tenderhearted, forgiving one another, just as God through Christ has forgiven you" (Eph. 4:31–32).

To the extent that we have experienced the grace of God, we will be able to forgive those who offend us. Or to put it the other way, if we're having a hard time forgiving someone, we need to dive deeper into the endless sea of God's love, grace, and forgiveness so we'll be filled and overflowing. Even then, it's not easy to forgive, but at least it's possible.

Choose to forgive your ex so your children will have an emotionally and spiritually healthy parent who is present and not haunted by the past.

6. Don't use your child as a weapon.

Don't withhold visitation rights just to infuriate your ex. Resist the urge to spoil your child to make the other parent look like "the bad guy." Don't pretend to be too busy to allow your child to receive a phone call. All forms of "parental alienation" are toxic. You may think you're winning the game, but your child is losing.

Don't use your child to be a "message mule" to communicate with your ex just because you don't want to talk to him or her. Don't play games, and don't use your child to avoid hard realities. Be an adult. Even though it's uncomfortable, have direct interaction with your ex when you need to.

7. Find common ground whenever possible.

It's inevitable and predictable that you and your ex-spouse won't agree on everything—or even many things. After all, your marriage ended because you couldn't find enough in common to stay together. After the divorce, you may disagree about your child's bedtimes, curfew, dating rules, diet, entertainment choices, and everything else imaginable.

Don't look for trouble. Don't fixate on a disagreement and blow it into World War III. Do all you can to stop the cycle of manipulation, game playing, and blame. It may not be easy to find common ground, but work hard to make it happen. Find regular times to talk to your ex—away from the ears of the children—to agree on rules and expectations.

Be flexible: Don't insist that the children be raised your way all the time, and limit your demands to a few things that are most important to you. For instance, you might be flexible about the child's bedtime when she's at your ex's house, but you may have strong convictions about not attending R-rated movies. If you agree to flexibility about going to bed, your ex may agree to restrictions about movies.

8. If your ex seems determined to undermine your wishes, don't take the bait.

Yes, it would be nice if everyone got along really well after a divorce. It happens sometimes, but more often hurt feelings and deep disappointments turn people into fighters. Don't fight back if your ex is determined to go against your wishes.

A lady's ex-husband told their preteen son, "When you get older, if you want to drink, that's fine. If you want to have sex with girls, that's great. All I ask is that you just do it in my house. I'll give you the upstairs. I'll go downstairs and watch television. I won't bother you at all. I just want to make sure you're safe."

The mother's values, hopes, and desires for her son are, to say the least, very different! What can she do about her ex's encouragement toward sin? How can she train her son according to the Word of God without tearing down the other parent?

The fact is that a parent can't control what goes on in the ex's home. You have to run your home like God wants you to run your home. If the child asks about the difference, share your opinion, along with your calm reasoning, without accusations . . . and pray. Pray like crazy! When children are old enough, they'll make their own choices. Your hope is that the seeds of God's Word you've sown in the child's life will bear fruit in the long run.

Message Fit

We've looked at a lot of perspectives and principles about helping children cope more effectively with the trauma of divorce. Obviously, we could address the specifics of each age range in far more detail, but these general guidelines give you plenty of handles. Younger children need fewer details and lots of hugs and attention. Older kids need more details, time to ask questions, and a strong heart as they process their powerful emotions. In addition to the difference in ages, children have different personalities, even from one sibling to another. Be observant, get input from competent, experienced friends or professionals, and tailor the message to your child. By all means, stay involved by showing lots of love. Your world has cratered, and so has theirs.

We haven't addressed the complicating factor of blended families. This brings far more opportunities for triangles to occur, leading to alliances, isolation, secrets, and manipulation. Again, anticipate the problems and address them before, during, and after the new marriage.

Always remember Peter's encouragement: "Most important of all, continue to show deep love for each other, for love covers a multitude of sins" (1 Peter 4:8). God's love covers your sins, your ex's sins, and your child's sins. More than ever, people who struggle through the excruciating pain of divorce need plenty of love.

Ron Deal, a respected author, speaker, and therapist, has written a number of excellent books on blended families, including *The Smart Stepfamily, The Smart Stepdad,* and *The Smart Stepmom.*

Chapter 7

How to Talk to Your Kids About Friendships

All of us know the importance of our kids selecting good friends. We see the impact of those choices every day. Some of us remember the bad decisions we made in picking friends, and we want to protect our kids from making similar mistakes. For a while—until our children go to school—we have almost total control over the selection of playmates for our children. We have decreasing control over them until they learn to drive, and then, it seems, we have very little control at all. At that point, we not only have no *control* over our kids' friends, we also have no *clue* about them!

Mark Entzminger, a close friend and the Senior Director of Children's Ministry for the Assemblies of God, teaches his son that there are three types of relationships: a leader, mentor, or pastor who pulls us up spiritually; peers who are on the same level spiritually; and those who are pulling us down. And conversely, we have one of those three effects in our various relationships. Mark's point isn't to label his son's friends, but to offer insight about the influence of his relationships. It only takes one or two people pulling us down to make a devastating impact. Solomon observed, "Walk with the wise and become wise; associate with fools and get in trouble" (Prov. 13:20). A similar contemporary insight says: "Show me your friends, and I'll show you your future." This statement is absolutely true.

One of the most important and challenging tasks of parents is to impart wisdom to their kids about choosing friends. The goal isn't to control their kids' decisions, but to teach them to make good choices on their own.

In my experience, the single most influential factor that starts young people down the wrong path is having "friends" in their lives who make a negative impact. I've seen kids mess up their lives because of wrong friends more than any other reason. But the problem isn't confined to children. I've watched young adults, single adults, and married people choose friends poorly. Consequently, they experience corroding influences and sometimes face devastating consequences. Paul warned us: "Don't be fooled . . . for 'bad company corrupts good character'" (1 Cor. 15:33).

Steering Your Kids

When your children are small, you can create an environment where they're with other kids who are pleasant and agreeable. As they grow up, your input will be more like a coach on the sidelines. Here are a few basic principles to help you steer your kids to good friends.

1. Set boundaries and expectations.

When your children are very young, you can go with them when they're invited to play with new friends. If you have any questions about the home where the other child lives, you can have the kids play at your house under your supervision.

As children get older (junior high and high school), you can set a curfew and establish clear expectations about acceptable behavior. Their understanding and "buy-in" are crucial, so do all you can to open a dialogue about the "house rules" instead of merely issuing demands. Of course, many teenagers push back on virtually all restrictions, even the ones they know are good and right. Don't react. Be clear, pleasant, and persistent, and be willing to bend a little from time to time when it's appropriate.

Part of the dialogue about parties, time with friends, and other social settings is honest conversation about kids' choices and the culture. One parent told her daughter, "Leave the party and come home if you're uncomfortable.

You don't have to give any excuses or reasons—to your friends or to me." She added, "If you're somewhere people are using drugs, drinking, or engaging in sexual practices, call me and I'll come get you—no questions asked."

2. Open dialogue.

From the time your kids are little and for the rest of their lives, have open, honest, insightful conversations about the meaning of friendships. Don't wait for a major catastrophe before you talk to them. Ask open-ended questions, but don't pry. When they get home from school, you might ask:

"Who was particularly nice to you today?"

"Was anyone unkind to someone else?"

"Did anyone make fun of anyone today?"

"Who made you feel good about yourself today?"

Depending on the response, you might simply say, "Tell me more about that," or, "How did that make you feel?"

> **From the time your kids are little and for the rest of their lives, have open, honest, insightful conversations about the meaning of friendships.**

Avoid being judgmental or giving advice. Your child is probably smart enough to read between the lines and sense your conclusions. This way, you give your child the responsibility and privilege of making appropriate evaluations about his or her friends.

One way to stimulate good conversation and shape your child's responses to situations before they occur is to ask "What if?" For instance, you can ask:

"What if you go to the party and someone offers you an alcoholic drink?"

"What if that really cute boy/girl wants to kiss you?"

"What if somebody asks to see your answers to a test?"

"What if someone dares you to jump off a bridge into the river?"

One mom and dad found these hypothetical questions so stimulating they thought of different ones to ask at dinner almost every night for a week. They knew the questions must be working well because their son started asked *them* some tough "What if" questions!

3. Provide feedback.

As the child moves through adolescence toward adulthood, continue to give feedback about relationships, but offer it sparingly. Look for patterns. You might say, "I've noticed that when you're with Bobby, you're not very happy. What's that about?" Or, "You invite some people over to our house to spend time with you, but you don't invite Janice. Tell me about that."

Simple observations—without emotion and without judgment—can open the door for wonderful conversations that allow you to give valuable feedback . . . not value statements about the friends, but dialogue about the impact of those friends on your child. If you criticize your child's friends, you'll almost certainly arouse a defensive response and shut down conversation. Instead, look for clear patterns and make honest, open, unemotional statements about how those relationships are affecting your child.

4. Don't overreact.

One mother came to me with tears in her eyes. She told me her eleven-year-old daughter was enamored with an eighteen-year-old girl who she thought was "super cool." The distraught mom explained, "The older girl has a tattoo, a pierced nose, dyed hair, and wears outrageous clothes!"

I asked, "Why do you think your daughter is attracted to the other girl?"

The mom answered, "Uh, I don't know. I guess she wants to look like her."

"Maybe," I answered, "or maybe she's trying to get a reaction from you."

The mom looked stunned, and then she smiled. "If that's what she's up to, I guess she succeeded!"

In an article on "Parenting Solutions: Bad Friends," Michele Borba explains that parents need to think before they leap to make assumptions:

> It's okay for your kid to have different kinds of friends. In fact, we should encourage those relationships. Exposing our kids to diversity is a big part of helping them broaden their horizons, develop tolerance and empathy, learn new habits, develop new perspectives, and get along with others. The trick here is to figure out when the other kid's values or lifestyle is really reckless, self-destructive, or totally inappropriate.[21]

5. Get outside input.

If you're concerned about one (or more) of your child's friends, get input from someone you trust: a fellow parent, your own parents, a teacher, a coach, or a pastor—preferably someone who knows both children, but who at least knows the other child. You want an objective appraisal, not just someone to confirm your deepest fears!

When it's possible, meet the parent(s) of the other child. You may find out that your suspicions about the child's home life are valid, or you may discover they're completely off base.

6. Make your home the safest place on earth.

Parenting is hard, but so is growing up. We often feel out of control as we raise our kids, but they feel the same way for very different reasons. When your kids are defiant, depressed, or anxious—especially for over an hour at a time—ask yourself, "What is my child feeling? What is she not getting that she needs right now?"

Often, as we look beneath the surface we discover hurts and needs that explain a child's aberrant behavior. There are, of course, many reasons a child may gravitate toward a particular individual or group of friends. She may be enthralled by a loud and unruly kid at school for the sheer excitement of being with a "rebel." Or he may feel bullied, and a gang offers protection. Some kids are looking for acceptance and love because they don't feel safe at home. Others find friends with the same interests and activities.

I'm not suggesting that your child's poor choice of friends is your fault, but a safe, warm, honest, respectful home environment provides many opportunities for hurts to be healed, wisdom to be imparted, and love to be shared. That's the kind of home where kids learn the value of true friendship.

When children feel like they have no friends, a grandparent's unconditional, warm, overflowing affection can make a big difference in their outlook on life.

7. Issue warnings sparingly.

Warnings are certainly warranted at times, but don't start or stay there. It can become a habit; some parents hardly talk to their kids unless they're warning them about something. I understand those parents are worried to death that their kids are at risk by trusting untrustworthy people, and they want to do anything possible to prevent them from destroying their lives.

> **Even when you warn your child about choosing the right friends, paint two pictures: one of potential negative consequences and another of the positive results that can result from making a different decision.**

Far more often, use the tools of dialogue and feedback to engage your children in conversation. As they get older, show respect for their right to choose. Even when you warn your child about choosing the right friends, paint two pictures: one of potential negative consequences and another of the positive results that can result from making a different decision. Offer love, hope, and a better vision for the future—especially after a child has chosen poorly.

In the Old Testament when God's people were ruining their lives in disobedience, God reminded them that He loved them and was waiting to restore their futures. Give the same assurance to your child when you feel compelled to issue a warning about his or her choice of friends.

The Right Kinds of Friends

Far too often, parents have only a vague idea of how to teach their kids about friendships. They can point to the obvious examples of the most disobedient and rebellious at one extreme and the most popular at the other. But even those categories of "worst" and "best" can be misleading. Sometimes the most popular kids are arrogant, secretly insecure, and manipulative!

We could look to popular culture to find the characteristics of good friends, but we would almost certainly be misled. Instead, let's look at some people in the Bible who exemplify the qualities of a good friend. Our kids need friends like these—and in fact, *we* need friends like these!

Our kids need a friend like Nathan who will tell them the truth. [22]

One of the first Bible stories our kids learn is about David killing the giant, Goliath. The event launched David's military career, but then he had to run for his life because King Saul became so jealous of his popularity. Finally, after years of running and fighting, David became king of Judah and then of all of Israel.

When his army was on the march and engaging the enemy, King David should have been leading them, but he decided to stay in Jerusalem. One day he was walking on his roof and saw a beautiful woman at a nearby house. He wanted to know who she was, so he had one of his servants summon her to his house. King David fell in love with this woman even though she was married. Their illicit relationship threatened to be exposed when she became pregnant.

The woman's husband was a soldier named Uriah, one of the men who had fought at David's side during the years he had to flee from Saul. David didn't care about Uriah's loyalty to him, and David's lust was far stronger than his loyalty to Uriah. David ordered Uriah to leave the battle and return to Jerusalem to give him a report. He figured Uriah would sleep with his wife and later assume the baby was his, but Uriah refused to go to his own house while his fellow soldiers continued to fight.

After his first plan failed, David tried another way to hide his sin. He told his general to send Uriah into the fiercest part of the battle and then have the other soldiers withdraw. As David planned, Uriah was killed, but so were several other of his soldiers. After David had Uriah killed, he married his wife.

David assumed he had gotten away with several horrible sins: adultery, murder, and the senseless deaths of loyal soldiers in his army. It was, from his point of view, a secret. But God knew.

God sent David's friend, the prophet Nathan, to confront the king. Nathan had a difficult decision: if he didn't speak to David about his sin, he would be disobeying God. However, if he confronted the king, a man who had already killed to keep a secret, Nathan would be risking his own life!

Nathan realized that speaking the truth to David was absolutely necessary—to honor God and to give David a chance to repent. The truth can hurt, and speaking the truth can be risky, but Nathan carefully planned how to touch the king's heart. He told David a story:

> "There were two men in a certain town. One was rich, and one was poor. The rich man owned a great many sheep and cattle. The poor man owned nothing but one little lamb he had bought. He raised that little lamb, and it grew up with his children. It ate from the man's own plate and drank from his cup. He cuddled it in his arms like a baby daughter. One day a guest arrived at the home of the rich man. But instead of killing an animal from his own flock or herd, he took the poor man's lamb and killed it and prepared it for his guest." (2 Sam. 12:1-4)

After he heard the story, King David was furious. He said, "As surely as the Lord lives, any man who would do such a thing deserves to die! He must repay four lambs to the poor man for the one he stole and for having no pity" (2 Sam. 12:5–6).

Nathan's story had the impact he hoped it would have on David. The king was outraged at the selfishness of the rich man in Nathan's story. At that moment, Nathan looked at David and told him, "You are that man! The LORD, the God of Israel, says: I anointed you king of Israel and saved you from the power of Saul. I gave you your master's house and his wives and the kingdoms of Israel and Judah. And if that had not been enough, I would have given you much, much more. Why, then, have you despised the word of the LORD and done this horrible deed? For you have murdered Uriah the Hittite with the sword of the Ammonites and stolen his wife" (2 Sam. 12:7–9).

David responded with a broken heart, "I have sinned against the LORD" (2 Sam. 12:13).

Why did Nathan confront the most powerful man in the kingdom? Did he have a death wish? No, of course not. Nathan wanted David to experience God's forgiveness— forgiveness so deep and wide that it washes away the sins of adultery and murder.

Why would Nathan carefully construct a story to capture David's heart instead of blasting him with the truth? Nathan's goal wasn't just to tell the truth, but to tell it in a way that touched David's heart and motivated him to repent.

One of a parent's tasks is to help kids value people like Nathan, and also, to become more like Nathan in their friendships—speaking the truth, often the hard truth, so friends will be warned. For that to happen, we need a passionate devotion to truth in our marriages and our friendships. If our kids don't have at least one or two brave, loving friends like Nathan was to David, they may drift into selfish, destructive behaviors. We all need friends like this if we're going to walk with God in grace and truth.

Speaking the truth with grace is risky, but it's powerful. Solomon realized sparks often fly when friends are honest with each other. He wrote, "As iron sharpens iron, so a friend sharpens a friend" (Prov. 27:17).

> **If our kids don't have at least one or two brave, loving friends like Nathan was to David, they may drift into selfish, destructive behaviors.**

Our kids need a friend like Barnabas who will encourage them.

In Luke's account of the early church in Acts, we find a man named Joseph—but the disciples called him Barnabas, which means "Son of Encouragement." Our kids need someone like him in their lives.

I ran in a marathon in 2013. At various points I was exhausted, and I thought I would die! Somewhere past the midway point, I thought I had "hit the wall" of the limit of my endurance as my muscles ached and my mind wandered. I managed to run a few more miles, when suddenly

I saw a beautiful sight. Cherith, Ashton, and Jordan, along with my mom and stepdad, were waving and cheering like crazy! I could hear them yelling, "You're going to make it!" "We're with you!" "You can do it!" "You're almost there!" With their encouragement, I was able to cross the finish line. Many other people who run in marathons confess to being so tired they feel like giving up in the latter parts of the race, but encouragement helps them make it.

Barnabas was an amazing friend and encourager. In the earliest days of the church, a lot of new believers were in Jerusalem, far from home and without provisions. To help care for them, Barnabas sold a field and gave the money to the apostles. He didn't wait to be asked. He saw a need, and he stepped up to help his friends.

If your children are struggling with their grades, they need a friend who will step up to help them study. If your children forget their lunch money, they need a friend who will share a lunch or loan them some money. If your children are struggling to make new friends, they need one good friend who will introduce them to others. Whatever the need, your children need a friend like Barnabas who will step up to help. That's what an encourager does.

Barnabas became a trusted friend of one of the most influential men of all time: the apostle Paul. Paul had been a fierce opponent of Christians, hunting them down, capturing, and killing them, but Jesus met him and changed his life. When Paul arrived in Jerusalem, many believers were naturally still afraid of him. They wondered if his "conversion" was a trick to get inside and arrest more of them. At that critical moment in Paul's life, Barnabas stood up for him. With Barnabas's support, Paul became an incredible spokesman for Christ and carried the message of the gospel to the whole Roman world!

Our kids need a friend or two like Barnabas, people who will stand by them even when others don't believe in them.

Our kids need a friend like Silas who will sing with them in the dark.

Silas was another friend and partner of Paul's who accompanied him on some of his missionary journeys to the continent of Europe. When the two of them arrived at the Roman city of Philippi, they encountered a slave girl who was possessed by a demon that enabled her to predict the future. Her owners were making a lot of money from her ability, but she also kept yelling out to people about the mission of Paul and Silas. After several days of being interrupted by her shouting, Paul cast out the demon. Were the girl's owners happy that she was healed? Not at all! Now they had no source of income, so they seized Paul and Silas and had them stripped, beaten, and thrown into prison. The jailer put them in the deepest, darkest part of the dungeon and fastened them securely in wooden stocks.

Sometimes we assume that if we walk with God, the Lord will make everything smooth and easy for us. I think Paul and Silas would have a different understanding of the consequences of following Christ. Even though they had been doing God's will, they suffered the epitome of a really bad day! Yet in the dungeon, these two men gave new meaning to the concept of "the bonds of friendship."

Silas was the kind of friend our kids need in times of trouble and heartache—someone who will sing with them in life's darkest moments.

In tough times, most people whine and complain. Silas and Paul had a different response. In the darkness of the dungeon that night, the other prisoners heard a strange sound. It was singing! A short time later, God sent a miracle. Luke tells us what happened:

> Around midnight Paul and Silas were praying and singing hymns to God, and the other prisoners were listening. Suddenly, there was a massive earthquake, and the prison was shaken to its foundations. All the doors immediately flew open, and the chains of every prisoner fell off! The jailer woke up to see the prison doors wide open. (Acts 16:25–27)

Silas was the kind of friend our kids need in times of trouble and heartache—someone who will sing with them in life's darkest moments. When things are going wrong, our children don't need friends who will complain, fuss, and whine about how bad things are. They need friends who will lift them up and remind them that God is in control.

When our kids find friends who continue to believe God in times of heartache, God often does amazing things. In Philippi that night, He caused an earthquake that led to the release (though not the escape) of the prisoners, the salvation of the jailer and his family, and the spread of the church to a new city. Then and now, God works through the tenacious, singing, optimistic faith of friends to provide hope, renewed faith, and courage to keep trusting God's goodness and power.

Our kids need friends like the "Fantastic Four" who will bring them closer to Jesus.

Mark's gospel (2:1–12) describes the love, creativity, and loyalty of four amazing friends. Another friend of theirs had been paralyzed for years. When they heard Jesus was coming to their community, they decided to take their friend to Him to be healed. But there was a problem: the house was so crowded they couldn't get in!

When they saw they couldn't get in the front door, they climbed up to the roof, cut a hole in it, and lowered the friend (still on his mat) down into the middle of the room right in front of Jesus. I can imagine Jesus looking up and smiling as pieces of the roof and ceiling fell on Him. I don't believe He minded at all. He saw the faith of the four friends, healed the paralyzed man so he could walk, and forgave him so he would have something even more valuable than mobility—eternal life.

Our kids need friends who are willing to do whatever it takes to bring them closer to Jesus.

Our kids need a friend like Paul who is further along on the spiritual journey.

The apostle Paul was one of the greatest leaders in history. One of the most touching relationships in Paul's life was with a young man named Timothy. Paul taught him about God, spiritual life, and leadership. In fact, the Bible contains two letters Paul wrote to Timothy; the second one is the last letter Paul wrote before the Romans executed him.

Your kids are like Timothy, and they need a friend and mentor like Paul, someone who is further along on the spiritual journey and can help them grow in their faith. Your child probably has a lot of peer friendships, but this is a different kind of relationship. A "Paul" is someone who is probably a little older and certainly wiser in understanding how life works—and someone who cares enough to impart wisdom to your child. People who might play this important role could be youth ministry volunteers, a "big brother" in the community or the church, a coach or an assistant coach, an aunt, an uncle, or a grandparent.

Does your child have a Paul? Do you?

Our kids need a friend like Timothy to help them become better Christians.

Like all meaningful relationships, Paul and Timothy's friendship had a mutual benefit: Paul was willing to give, and Timothy was willing to receive. In fact, Timothy was hungry for Paul's love and leadership. He was humble enough to realize he needed a friend like Paul to speak into his life and help him become the man God wanted him to be.

I believe it's a maxim of life that we learn the most when we lead others. When placed in a position of leadership, we realize what we know, but more importantly, what we don't know. So we pay closer attention, we soak up wisdom, and we pray that our words and actions will make a difference in the lives of those who are following us.

Your kids, even the quiet ones, can become trusted, gifted, effective leaders who shape the lives of others around them. Your children may not know everything, but as you pour yourself into them, they can pour themselves into others. The relationship may be formal, like a school mentoring program for younger kids, but it will probably be informal as they earn the respect of their friends.

Our kids need a friend like Nehemiah who will inspire them to do great things.

Our culture is focused on the acquisition of two things: personal peace, and affluence—not the kind of peace that Jesus gives as we trust Him in the middle of life's storms but the absence of any storms at all, and then plenty of money and possessions to make life comfortable. Is that "the abundant Christian life" you hear so many televangelists teach about?

It's easy to become absorbed with simply making life work and enjoying as much as you can. Certainly, God gives us all kinds of blessings to enjoy, but they're always given to us for a bigger purpose. From God's covenant with Abraham through the New Testament and today, "we are blessed to be a blessing." Jesus put it another way: "When someone has been given much, much will be required in return; and when someone has been entrusted with much, even more will be required" (Luke 12:48).

Our kids need to hang out with friends who are beginning to grasp that God has called them to be and do magnificent things for His glory.

Many Christians, young and old, are like spiritual zombies—going through the motions of daily life with no real purpose or meaning. They're spiritually asleep. The world is waiting for God's people to stand up in the middle of emptiness and heartache and point to the God who wants to do great things! Our kids need to hang out with friends who are beginning to grasp that God has called them to be and do magnificent things for His glory.

Heroes often surface during times of suffering and hopelessness. One of these instances took place after the Babylonians tore the city of Jerusalem to the ground and carried God's people into exile. The Israelites lived in a foreign land for decades, and their situation appeared bleak. But then the Persians defeated the Babylonians and the new leaders were willing to let the Jewish people return home. At that point, Nehemiah went to the Persian king and asked permission to return and rebuild the walls of Jerusalem. The king did better than that; he also gave Nehemiah all the resources he would need to accomplish the task.

When Nehemiah arrived in Jerusalem, he found the people demoralized and helpless. He told them, "You know very well what trouble we are in. Jerusalem lies in ruins, and its gates have been destroyed by fire. Let us rebuild the wall of Jerusalem and end this disgrace" (Neh. 2:17)!

Hadn't they seen the broken walls for years? Yes, of course. Hadn't they longed for their city to return to its glory? Definitely. But none of them had the vision, the compassion, and the heart to lead the effort to make it happen—until Nehemiah.

Nehemiah faced all kinds of challenges, including personal threats on his life, but he led the people in this important project. When they finished, Nehemiah inspected the walls. It was an amazing moment. Together, with the strength of God, they had done what no one thought possible.

Your kids need someone like Nehemiah to challenge them out of their complacency, show them the desperate needs around them, and enlist them to participate in the great work of redeeming the world for Jesus Christ.

You Matter!

Perhaps you've heard the widespread assumption that parents lose any influence over their children by the time they reach adolescence. Don't believe it. Recent research shows that presumption is false.

Chris Knoester was the lead author of the Ohio State University study of 11,483 kids and their parents. Peers may take up most of our kids' time, but parents are still the most influential factor in their development. A strong, healthy, supportive relationship with parents leads to many positive outcomes, including the ability to choose good friends, the skill to set boundaries in relationships, and the hope for a brighter future.[23]

Raising your children is one of the most fulfilling yet challenging tasks of your life. It's often a struggle, but don't give up. Get the help you need. Other parents have traveled the same road, and they have a world of wisdom to share with you. If things get really tough, seek the help of a competent counselor to steer you in the right direction.

Your relationship with your child matters. And you're never alone. Ask God to give you His wisdom, strength, and timing to speak words of life and hope into your child's life. God delights in you and in your child. Struggles are opportunities to trust Him more than ever, and He is always faithful.

Chapter 8

How to Talk to Your Kids About Money

Money is one of the most common and most intense sources of stress for individuals and families. In fact, disagreement about money is the number one cause of divorce. Kansas State University researcher Sonya Britt observes, "Arguments about money [are] by far the top predictor of divorce. It's not children, sex, in-laws or anything else. It's money—for both men and women."[24]

Surprisingly, the tension isn't usually about the lack of money; it's over different values and expectations about money. Most people, even among those in our churches,

were never taught how to manage money. When I ask people what they learned from their parents about money, I get
some very interesting answers:

Katie told me, "My mom and dad always had 'my money
and your money.' My dad kept tight controls on his
money, but my mom spent everything she had on things
we needed … and things we didn't need. My dad believed
money provided security. He placed a very high value on
it, but mom demonstrated that money was only valuable
when it gives you pleasure and relief. I watched all this
as I was growing up, and to be honest, it was pretty confusing. As an adult, I'm still trying to figure out the value
and meaning of money."

Rachel explained, "My parents didn't teach me anything
about managing money. They owned businesses that
were very successful, and so money wasnt a problem for
them. They spent whatever they wanted to spend. After
I left home and went out on my own, money became a
problem … a big problem. I've had to learn basic lessons
about making money, saving, giving, and spending, but
all these lessons are brand new to me. I didn't learn any
of this from my parents."

Rob told me, "My mother taught me how to 'rob Peter
to pay Paul,' as she called it. We never had much money,

and sometimes she didn't have enough to pay all the bills. At the end of many months when I was a child, she had to decide which bills to pay, what calls to make, and who to ignore until she got a demand letter. Playing this game seemed completely normal to her, but it sure didn't show me how to manage my finances."

Personally, I know my parents taught me about tithing and encouraged me to save, but those must have been rare and brief conversations because I don't remember any talks with them about how to handle money. My parents were brought up during an era when people believed, "Money is a personal thing. You don't talk about it."

At one point in high school, I asked my parents how much salary they made. Both of them blurted out in unison, "That's none of your business!" They were right. I didn't need to know their salaries, but they didn't need to act like I had just asked the CIA to reveal the nation's biggest secrets! Their words, the tone of voice, and the look on their faces shouted, "Money is off limits! Don't bring it up anymore!"

As I counsel with many families, I've discovered that my parents aren't alone in their discomfort talking about money. Many parents assume their kids will learn how to manage money by osmosis or magic. They don't. Children learn about money when their parents intentionally, persistently, and wisely impart knowledge, and as they model those principles in front of them.

My Goals

The Bible has a lot to say about money. In fact, Jesus said more about money than He did heaven and hell combined. Fifteen percent of His recorded teaching was about money. Why? Because Jesus knew that a person's view of money is a window to the soul. How we handle money demonstrates our deepest hopes and fears, our expectations, and the source of our security.

Many people get nervous when a pastor begins talking or writing about money. They assume his main motive is to get them to give as much as possible to the church. I want to assure you that you can relax. My goals are much broader and deeper than that:

- I want you and your children to understand God's view of money and to live in financial freedom instead of the slavery experienced by so many people in our culture. When we live according to God's values, we enjoy peace and security, and we avoid anxiety and instability.

- One of the ways God wants us to view money is to realize He owns it all, and He has entrusted wealth—a lot or a little—to us so that we are "blessed to be a blessing." In other words, we'll be glad to use every resource God gives us to build His kingdom and make a difference in the lives of other people. When we have that perspective, giving is a thrill, not guilt-driven torture.

- I want to assure you that no matter how badly you've managed your resources in the past, it's not too late to learn solid biblical principles and live by them. In most cases, parents will learn God's lessons about money at the same time they're imparting those lessons to their kids. Don't wait to start over!

Perceptions of Money—The World's Way

Every day we're bombarded with the world's values about everything: money, sex, beauty, success, comfort, acceptance, status, and anything else that people believe will bring meaning and happiness. The false perception of money is woven into our culture. If we look around for only a few minutes, we'll quickly see the world's misguided values about money:

1. Money is king.

Wealth, we're told in countless ways, is the key to happiness, fame, power, and friends. Money is king, so do whatever it takes to acquire more. The more you have, the better off you are. The more you make, the more important you are. But no matter how much you have, it's never enough. Someone else always has more, so there's another rung to climb on the ladder of success.

A young mother told me about the values instilled in her when she was a child: "I was taught from a very young age that money wasn't just something we needed in order to eat, sleep in a home, and have some things we needed. Money was far more important than that! To my parents, money was the central issue of their lives . . . like an idol, a god to be pursued and worshiped. No matter how much my dad made, it was never enough. He fought for a higher position in a company and pushed people out of the way to get a promotion and raise. He measured his identity by his income and possessions, so everything felt like a competition."

2. Spend every dime you make.

If acquiring things and pleasures is a person's highest value, he will spend every cent to get a nicer car, better clothes, a finer vacation, and anything else that will give him pleasure and prestige. The world says, "Money is made to be spent! You can't take it with you, so spend it all!"

People with this mindset are always thinking about the next purchase. No matter what they have, it's not enough. When they get paid, the money is as good as gone to things they've been planning to buy. When they get an unexpected inflow of cash from a bonus or a tax refund, they lick their lips and run out to buy something new. After all, it's "free money"!

3. Borrowing is completely normal.

One of the lost values of our culture is delayed gratification. Credit cards give people what they want now, with the vague commitment to pay later. In only a generation or two, the average amount of borrowed money among people has skyrocketed. Consumer debt used to be avoided like the plague, but today it's viewed as completely normal—and in fact, is highly valued because "it improves your credit score."

Many parents and their children see something they want and assume, "I've got to have it right now, even though I don't have the money for it. But that's okay because I have a credit card. I'll pay for it later . . . or at least, I'll make the minimum payments. That's good enough."

A study in 2014 showed that the average U.S. household credit card debt stands at $7,743 among those households with at least one credit card that carries a balance. In total, American consumers owe $11.62 trillion in debt: $880.3 billion in credit card debt and $8.05 trillion in mortgages.[25] Another study found that Americans have accumulated $1.2 trillion in student loans.[26]

The way we use money shows what we value. In fact, it reveals what our hearts love most and actually worship. In a famous commencement address at Kenyon College, David Foster Wallace described the foolishness of putting other pursuits in God's rightful place—the center of our lives:

If you worship money and things—if they are where you tap real meaning in life—then you will never have enough. Never feel you have enough. It's the truth. Worship your own body and beauty and sexual allure and you will always feel ugly, and when time and age start showing, you will die a million deaths before they finally plant you. . . . Worship power—you will feel weak and afraid, and you will need ever more power over others to keep the fear at bay. Worship your intellect, being seen as smart—you will end up feeling stupid, a fraud, always on the verge of being found out.[27]

The world's view of money promises thrills, security, and fulfillment, but it produces pride, fear, laziness, and anxiety. It is far better to consider another set of values and expectations, another kingdom and another King, and another way to perceive money. God's perspective promises what the world can't deliver. When we follow God's plan to earn, save, and give, we have peace, joy, and true security in the One who never changes, no matter what the stock market is doing.

Changing kingdoms isn't easy, but it's essential. We have choices every day to feed our minds with God's truth and then live in a way that honors Him. At each moment, we need insight to see the choice. Paul explained to the Christians in Rome: "Don't copy the behavior and customs of this world, but let God transform you into a new person by changing the way you think. Then you will learn to know God's will for you, which is good and pleasing and perfect" (Rom. 12:2).

Perceptions of Money—God's Way

One of the great blessings of my life is that I get to work with Rod Loy, my senior pastor and dear friend and mentor. Rod teaches clearly, powerfully, and attractively about God's values about money. When Rod planned to teach the families of our church how to use money God's way, he asked me to work with him and our creative team to create the sermons. I taught the children the same ideas and concepts Pastor Rod taught the adults. The concepts in this section are the product of our collaborative efforts. The principles are effective—not only for kids, but for their parents, too.

1. The Follow-the-Leader Principle

When you were a kid, do you remember playing "follow the leader" on the playground? Kids still play it. As a kids' pastor, I still get to play. It's even more fun now that I'm so much older and bigger than the kids. I have lots of fun climbing obstacles, spinning around, running and jumping, and being followed by a group of hysterically laughing children.

When it comes to life, and especially financial matters, it's important to make sure you're following the right leader. If you follow the wrong leader, you'll end up in the wrong place. Choose wisely. Paul wrote in Philippians, "Dear brothers and sisters, pattern your lives after mine, and learn from those who follow our example" (Phil. 3:17).

When it comes to money, who is the right leader? Of course, God is the leader of our lives in every area—including money. The Bible is our guidebook for living. In the pages of the Bible we find plenty of clear instructions for managing our money. We don't have to wonder about earning, saving, spending, giving, or debt. God tells us plainly how He has designed life to work.

Many people wonder why their finances are offtrack. It's like they wake up one day and are shocked they're in debt! No one needs to be surprised. The principle is clear: If you want God's blessings in your finances, follow God's instructions. Sadly, many people never make the connection between cause and effect regarding their money. They disobey God's instructions and wonder why they don't receive His blessings. They expect God to bless their disobedience.

If you want God's blessings in your finances, follow God's instructions.

Good parents never treat their kids that way. We don't bless our kids when they disobey. Instead, we lovingly withhold blessings as a consequence to teach them an important lesson. We use cause and effect in a positive way to bless them when they are obedient, and we use it to show them that disobedience is painful. Our goal isn't to punish or harm, but to motivate them to obey the next time.

The principle applies in every area of life. At the office, who gets promoted: the person who follows the boss's instructions or the person who doesn't? If you want the promotion or the raise, if you want blessings at work, follow the leader's instructions.

You can help teach your kids this principle by literally playing follow the leader. To demonstrate the concept, first be a fun leader and afterward ask them to describe their experience. Then play again and this time be a horrible leader! Walk them through mud puddles, have them close their eyes and stumble into pillows, and make them put their hands into something gross (but safe). After that game, ask them to describe their experience. Then explain that they have a choice of leaders when it comes to their money, too. They can follow the world's ideas of spending and debt and suffer the consequences, or they can follow God's plan and enjoy peace, security, and blessing.

2. The Library Principle

When we check a book out of the library, most of us take good care of it because we know it doesn't belong to us. We have it for a certain amount of time and for a particular purpose, but we don't own it.

The Library Principle acknowledges that everything we have is a gift from God. He's the owner; we just have it "on loan" for a while. The apostle Paul explained to the Corinthians that he and his friend Apollos were stewards of the message of the gospel: "So look at Apollos and me as mere servants of Christ who have been put in charge of explaining God's mysteries. Now, a person who is put in charge as a manager must be faithful" (1 Cor. 4:1–2).

God is the Creator and owner of everything in the universe. He has entrusted resources to us for a while. We are stewards. Like the book from the library, God has loaned the resources to us for a particular time and a specific purpose. If we understand this concept, it will change how we view everything in our possession.

When we believe, "I own my money and my stuff," we tend to make every decision based on our agenda, not God's. We see ourselves as owners, with the privilege of using everything to satisfy our desires. Actually, we may act in two different ways: Some of us spend the way we want to spend, borrow to fulfill our immediate wants, grudgingly pay bills, save very little, and resent paying taxes. Then, if we really feel good and there's a worthwhile cause, we might even give some to the church. Others are more interested in security than comfort, so they count every penny, save as much as possible, and worry about not having enough. These opposite views are signs of self-indulgence or self-reliance instead of trust in a good and generous God who entrusts us with resources to use for His kingdom.

Some people argue, "Hey, wait. I work hard for the money I make. If I earn it, it's mine." But who gives us the intelligence, talents, and opportunities to make money? God is the source of our ability to make money, so everything we earn is also a gift from Him.

As parents, we want our kids to realize that "every good and perfect gift comes from above" (James 1:17, NIV). We aren't owners; we're stewards of things God has entrusted to us.

3. The Simon Says Principle

Another game I loved to play when I was a kid was Simon Says. One person is "it" or "Simon," and gives instructions for others to follow, but only if "Simon says":

Simon says, "Sit down." They sit down.

Simon says, "Stand up." They stand.

Simon says, "Shout 'Hallelujah.'" And they shout.

"Turn around." If someone turns around, everyone else laughs because Simon didn't say to do it.

You win the game by doing what Simon says. If you do something Simon doesn't say, you're out. This is the principle of genuine and immediate obedience.

In every area of life, we have choices: God's way or our way, God's agenda or our agenda, God's timing or our timing, indulging ourselves or trusting God.

In every area of life, we have choices: God's way or our way, God's agenda or our agenda, God's timing or our timing, indulging ourselves or trusting God. Like the game, if we follow God's commands, we win; if we don't, we lose. In this case, we have the added assurance that the leader we follow is infinitely wise, loving, and strong. We can trust that He knows best, even if what He says makes us uncomfortable or doesn't seem to make sense to us at the time.

One of the most familiar passages of Scripture about money is found in the writing of the prophet Malachi. The people had been selfish and disobedient with their money. God pleaded with them to trust Him and accused them, "Should people cheat God? Yet you have cheated me!" God then said,

> "But you ask, 'What do you mean? When did we ever cheat you?' You have cheated me of the tithes and offerings due to me. You are under a curse, for your whole nation has been cheating me. Bring all the tithes into the storehouse so there will be enough food in my Temple. If you do,' says the Lord of Heaven's Armies, 'I will open the windows of heaven for you. I will pour out a blessing so great you won't have enough room to take it in! Try it! Put me to the test!'" (Mal. 3:8–10)

The tithe is 10 percent of a person's income. If it seems like an exorbitant amount of money to give to God, then we don't have a good grasp on the wonder of His grace toward us. We were helpless and hopeless, without God and without any way to repair the problem sin had caused. God didn't turn His back on us and walk away. Jesus Christ stepped out of the splendor of heaven to pay the price we couldn't pay. We deserved death, but He paid the debt for us. As we begin to understand His infinite gift to us, we won't begrudge giving Him anything He asks us to give. The tithe is just the starting point of obeying God—the first 10 percent of your income goes to Him, but there's no limit on how much we may give as we experience more of His grace and see how He uses our giving to transform lives.

Help younger kids understand the tithe by showing them a stack of $1 bills. Have them pretend that they were given $10 for Christmas or allowance. Take one bill out and place it to the side. The dollar, you can explain, is the tithe; it belongs to God. We give it to the church to help spread the gospel of Jesus in our city, state, country, and world.

Then show your children a stack of ten $10 bills. Help them understand that if they had $100, the tithe would be $10. Most children don't think in proportions. For them (and maybe for us) it's easier to think about giving God one dollar than to give Him ten dollars. The bigger the amount, the harder it seems it is for us to "let go."

Teach your kids that it's not about the amount; it's about the percentage. When God says something, we want to obey—not out of guilt, but in response to His love and sacrifice to save us.

Teach your kids this principle by playing Simon Says. Then open the Bible and look at what God says. You win when you do what He says.

4. The Leftovers Principle

Some people say tithing is important to them, but their budget doesn't reflect that commitment. Here is what happens: The world's values eat away at our thoughts and values. We want to give a tithe, but we also want some new clothes, a new car, or regular meals out at nice restaurants with friends. At the end of the month, we can barely pay our bills. We feel guilty enough to dig deep into our pockets to find a few dollars to put in the offering plate, but our hearts aren't in it. We forget that we are stewards of God's gifts and are following the rightful King. Instead of honoring Him by giving generously, we give Him only what little is left. Our prayer is, "God, I wish I could do more, but this is all I have. Oh Lord, please accept my leftovers."

Here's how I explain this principle to my kids: "I invite you over for dinner, take you to the dining room, show you to your seat, and dinner is served. I walk into the kitchen and come back with a plate of week-old meatloaf. (It might even have a little green mold on it.) How special would you feel? It certainly would be a horrible way for me to show you honor, wouldn't it?"

Instantly and completely, kids understand that treating a guest this way is unacceptable. I then explain that we treat

God this way when we don't put giving to Him into our regular financial plans.

Encourage your kids not to give God leftovers. "If we give," your kids may ask, "what will happen when we don't have enough for us?" Great question. Jesus explained that we can trust God to provide all we need:

> "So don't worry about these things, saying, 'What will we eat? What will we drink? What will we wear?' These things dominate the thoughts of unbelievers, but your heavenly Father already knows all your needs. Seek the Kingdom of God above all else, and live righteously, and he will give you everything you need." (Matt. 6:31–33)

Seek God first, and He promises to take care of the rest. Don't treat Him like an unwanted guest. Don't give Him your leftovers. Give the King your very best!

5. The Sam Walton Principle

Sam Walton was a brilliant businessman who founded Walmart, one of the most successful companies of all time. By the time he died, Walton was worth billions of dollars. However, if you saw him, you would never guess he was wealthy. Until the day he died, Sam still drove his old pickup and dressed in ordinary clothes—probably bought off the discount racks at one of his own stores. At some point earlier in his life, he learned the secret of living *below* his means.

He could afford to live extravagantly, but he chose to live modestly.

We live in a crazy world. People are obsessed with living large—having the biggest and the best of everything. When we get a clear picture of reality, we realize this pursuit is absurd. Actor Will Smith once noted, "Too many people spend money they haven't earned, to buy things they don't need, to impress people they don't like."

When Rod Loy was twelve years old, his father taught him the principle of living below his means. Rod's first job was mowing lawns. He wasn't old enough to drive a car, so he towed his lawnmower behind his bicycle, knocked on doors, and asked if the homeowner needed his yard mowed. Rod's father gave him a financial plan: The first 10 percent went to God. Rod never questioned it and never departed from it. His dad told him he could spend 50 percent of what he made on absolutely anything he wanted: baseball cards, ice cream, candy, video games, movies, or whatever. The other 40 percent was to go into savings.

Rod followed this plan for many years. Every week, 10 percent (or more) went to God, 40 percent went into savings, and he spent the rest on anything that he wanted. By the time Rod got married, he had more money saved than you can imagine!

As Rod looked back, he reflected, "Over the years, the percentages have shifted. Today I give more to God than ever before. Now that I have a family, putting food in the fridge and gas in the car costs a little more, but I still don't spend everything I make. I still save a big percentage. I don't live *within* my means; I live *below* my means. I can't tell you the peace that brings me. I don't ever have to worry about paying the bills or getting caught in a financial pinch. I also have freedom to help people anytime God puts someone on my heart."

Rod's dad taught him the secret to financial freedom. Put God first, then spend less than you make. It's that simple and that profound. Every week, every month, and every year, spend less than you make. Live below your means.

Why is it so important to follow this principle? Because you never know what emergencies may arise. Spending less than you make allows you to save for life's unexpected events: sickness, car accidents, home repairs, weddings, spontaneous trips, and anything else that may come up. In addition, having savings in the bank gives you the freedom to obey God's will for your life. Many people feel called by God to go to the mission field, but are so far in debt they can't go. That's so sad. Teach your kids to live below their means—and let them see you live that way—so they'll have the freedom to follow God whenever and wherever He leads them.

What are some steps to live below your means? First, write a budget. Look at your income and expenses, and lower your expenses to be less than your income. Yes, you may have to trim some things that you've considered "essential," but you won't die if you don't have the latest and greatest technology. In fact, you'll really live when you have financial freedom! When you get a raise or a bonus, don't rush out to spend it. Instead, live off the old salary instead of the new one and save the difference. With each raise, live by the previous salary. Within a few years, you'll be amazed how much you'll be able to give and save—all because you live below your means.

How do you teach your kids this principle? Follow the example of Rod's dad. Give your kids a plan to earn money, give money, save money, and spend money. You can't start too young! Give them an allowance and help them figure out percentages: the first 10 percent to God, a percentage to save, and the rest to spend.

> **Give your kids a plan to earn money, give money, save money, and spend money. You can't start too young!**

6. The Piggy Bank Principle

In a world of immediate gratification and consumer debt, we've lost the concept of saving money. The Piggy Bank Principle is about the importance of putting money in savings and letting it grow over time. Solomon observed, "Wealth from get-rich-quick schemes quickly disappears; wealth from hard work grows over time" (Prov. 13:11).

Teach your children the Piggy Bank Principle by matching what they save. When each of my kids, Ashton and Jordan, saved their first $50, I matched it and opened a savings account in their name. I told them, "Here's my commitment: I'll match every dollar you put into this account. You put in a dollar, and I'll put in a dollar. You'll double your money on the day you put it in the account, and all of it then earns interest. But this is a long-term savings account. You won't even see this money until after you graduate from college. At that point, you can use it to buy a car, make a down payment on a house, start a business, or get married." They didn't start out with much, but if they keep putting a little at a time into that account, by the time they graduate from college they'll have a good nest egg.

7. The Veruca Salt Principle

Do you remember Veruca Salt? She was the spoiled little brat in *Willie Wonka and the Chocolate Factory* who wanted everything right now! At one point, she demanded, "I want that golden goose, Daddy! And I want it *now*!" This principle contrasts her attitude with the importance of delayed gratification, which means, "I'll sacrifice and wait now, and get it later." Solomon wrote, "A person without self-control is like a city with broken-down walls" (Prov. 25:28).

When my friend Tyler was a boy, his family wanted a new television, but his dad wouldn't let them get one right away. Instead, they started saving money to buy it. Meanwhile, they studied the different kinds of televisions so they could make the best purchase. While their television savings account grew, they went to stores and looked at dozens of models, and they did research on the Internet. By the time they had enough money for one, they also had enough information to buy the right one. Since they were paying cash, they even negotiated a discount. Tyler said his family really enjoyed their new, paid-for-with-cash television.

One of the biggest benefits of living by the Veruca Salt Principle is that you avoid impulse buying. Impulse buying is often regret buying. When you wait, you often realize you don't even want the thing you thought you needed.

People who hear this principle sometimes complain, "It's no fun to wait!" Yes, waiting is difficult. It's a discipline we find throughout the Scriptures and in the lives of successful, mature people everywhere, but it requires forward thinking, insight, and commitment. For our kids to understand this principle, they need to see us demonstrate it. So practice it, and let them see you wait and save for something you want.

8. The Debt Monster Principle

One of the ways I taught my kids about the destructive nature of debt was by introducing them to a character we call the Debt Monster. I told them, "If you were walking down the street and there was a horrible beast on the loose around the corner, would you want someone to warn you? Of course! Well, there is a monster like that! It's a horrible beast called the Debt Monster. Don't look now, but he's right around the corner."

That usually gets their attention, and then I explain, "You're too young to be attacked by the Debt Monster, but let me show you what it looks like." I pull out a credit card and show it to them. "That's it! Be careful. It bites! It promises to make you happy, but it makes you poor, worried, and enslaved."

At that point, kids almost always ask, "How can that happen?" Depending on the age of the child, I may explain, "Credit cards make people think they can get whatever they want whenever they want it, but they don't realize they still have to pay for it later. When the bill comes due, they've already bought something else, and something else, and they fall deeper into the Debt Monster's mouth! Many people don't know it, but when you buy something with a credit card, you're actually borrowing money from the bank that sponsors the credit card. For every month you don't pay it back, they charge you 'interest,' which is one of the Debt Monster's biggest weapons. The interest rate on credit cards is high, and in some cases, astronomical! It's often 13 to 16 percent, but if a person is late making a monthly payment, the rate may increase to over 30 percent. Paying late or missing a payment adds extra fees to the bill each month."

In a *Forbes Magazine* article, Luke Landes explains, "Even if you avoid extra fees, an interest fee will be added to what you owe the following month. Interest adds up quickly, and could make a $100 purchase cost $200 in total or more rather quickly. When this happens, it's more than just time-shifting; it's as if waiting to watch your 30-minute recorded show would require 60 minutes of your life."[28]

All of this would be bad enough, but remember the Library Principle: It's all God's money, and we're just borrowing it. Any money that goes to the Debt Monster is God's money! Debt eats away our money, our joy, our freedom, and our future.

Teach your kids to stay away from the Debt Monster. Have them choose something they want to buy or do, or determine an amount they want to give, and then save together as a family. Even if you can afford it right now, don't rush out and buy it. Put a savings jar on your kitchen table and add money to it every week. When you have enough, go get the thing you've saved for, and enjoy every part of the process.

For many people today, paying cash instead of using credit is a different way of thinking. Waiting until you have the money to purchase something requires discipline. These practices, though, bring great freedom and peace of mind.

9. The Happy-and-You-Know-It Principle.

You've heard the phrase, "Money can't buy happiness." It's true. No amount of money or possessions will bring you true happiness. A friend told me a story about her father's persistent discontent. She said, "I learned from my dad that money can't buy happiness. But I learned this lesson the hard way because he had a lot but was never satisfied."

In our culture, people assume that contentment comes from having the next big thing. When we get something new, we feel thrilled, but only for a short while. Then we need something else, something bigger, something more. God has made us so that nothing external can ever give us true joy and contentment. But Paul explained that he had learned a valuable secret, the secret of contentment:

Not that I was ever in need, for I have learned how to be content with whatever I have. I know how to live on almost nothing or with everything. I have learned the secret of living in every situation, whether it is with a full stomach or empty, with plenty or little. For I can do everything through Christ, who gives me strength. (Phil. 4:11–13)

The secret of contentment is found in the knowledge that God is our constant and faithful source of love, peace, joy, and strength. Thanks to Him, we can enjoy His blessings and face obstacles with a full and contented heart.

> **The secret of contentment is found in the knowledge that God is our constant and faithful source of love, peace, joy, and strength.**

Do you remember that song, "If You're Happy and You Know It"? I love watching four year olds sing it. They know what this song is all about. They really *are* happy and content! Why? They haven't yet learned to compare themselves to others or worry about the future.

Comparison ruins contentment. When our kids get older, they're thrilled with their new phone and all its cool features . . . until they see a slightly newer phone in the hands of one of their friends. All of a sudden, they feel like a loser.

Let's be honest. Not being satisfied isn't just a problem for our teens. When we compare jobs, cars, hairstyles, hairlines, shoes, houses, awards, bonuses, and everything else imaginable, we feel either arrogant if we're doing better than others or ashamed if we aren't. Neither of those responses reflects the abundant life Jesus promised!

Teach your kids to stop comparing by not talking about what others have and what you don't have . . . or what you have that others don't have. Teach them to be content—truly happy—with whatever God has given you.

10. The Santa Claus Principle

This is the principle of *planned* generosity. I'm not suggesting we teach our kids that Santa is real. I have another point in using this metaphor: The generosity of Santa Claus teaches a vital principle in a way your children can understand—no matter if your children are two or twenty.

As the tradition goes, Santa delivers toys to all the girls and boys all over the world on Christmas Eve. Popular movies show his elves working hard all year to make the toys. Santa isn't taken by surprise on December 24 when it's time to load the sleigh. He doesn't wake up that morning and say, "Oh no, I've got to deliver toys all around the world, and I don't have any ready!" Instead, Santa works and plans all year for the big event.

In the same way, we won't be as generous as we hope to be unless we plan well. If we budget to give, we'll probably give wisely and generously. If we don't, we'll give only leftovers or nothing at all.

Teach your children to "budget generosity." This will enable them to obey God's voice. When He points out someone's need, they can give. When He directs, they will be ready.

How much do you budget? It changes with the seasons of life, but even if it's only $5 a week, budget to be generous. The Lord loves a generous heart. Moses instructed the people (and Paul echoed his challenge in a letter to the Corinthians): "Give generously to the poor, not grudgingly, for the LORD your God will bless you in everything you do" (Deut. 15:10; 2 Cor. 9:7–8).

11. The Parent Principle

God delights when we give like He has given to us: generously, intentionally, gladly, and sacrificially. One historian commented that only a few decades ago, our culture experienced a titanic shift from self-sacrifice to self-indulgence. Today we applaud the sacrifice of our troops and first responders, but most of the people in our society have no intention of sacrificing anything!

In teaching our kids about money, the concept of sacrifice is essential, but you and I have a head start. I call it the Parent Principle because most parents naturally and tenaciously sacrifice for their kids. In the same way, we need to learn to sacrifice at least some of our pleasures for the greater good, to build God's kingdom.

Cherith and I want a lot of things, but we know we can't have them all. We're not bitter about it. We gladly sacrifice those things so we can provide for Ashton and Jordan. We're not angry when Jordan drinks $15 worth of milk every week and eats everything that isn't nailed down. We're not resentful when their feet keep growing and they need new shoes every six weeks. We're not upset when they need uniforms for school, supplies for projects, money to eat out. Providing for children is expensive, but we're glad to do it even if it means we don't get some things we'd like for ourselves. We understand that's part of parenting.

For example, Cherith and I have always wanted a pool for our house, but we've put it off because we wanted to save money for our kids' college tuition. We don't want them to start off in life with a mountain of school loans and debt, so we've chosen to give up something we want for a bigger, better goal: a paid-for college education for our children.

Parents sacrifice because they want the best for their children. It's not an accidental sacrifice. It's intentional. It's a decision we make every day.

In handling money, all of us are called to forego some things we want for the sake of a bigger goal. Paul explained this concept in a letter to the Corinthians:

> Now I want you to know, dear brothers and sisters, what God in his kindness has done through the churches in Macedonia. They are being tested by many troubles, and they are very poor. But they are also filled with abundant joy, which has overflowed in rich generosity. For I can

testify that they gave not only what they could afford, but far more. And they did it of their own free will. They begged us again and again for the privilege of sharing in the gift for the believers in Jerusalem. (2 Cor. 8:1–4)

The people of Macedonia were dirt poor, but their love and joy in Christ propelled them to sacrifice gladly so the gospel could go out to more people. They sacrificed, but not for nothing. They sacrificed so that more people could experience the love, forgiveness, and acceptance of Jesus Christ.

Teach your kids to give up some things they want in order to give others what they need.

Teach your kids to give up some things they want in order to give others what they need.

Cherith and I wanted to plant the seeds of sacrifice in our kids. We asked Ashton and Jordan to give up something they really wanted so they could give the money to help others. On Christmas Day a few years ago, we had just finished opening presents and the kids were anticipating playing with their new toys. Cherith and I explained that some people were feeling lonely that day, and we could take them some joy. We loaded up the car, drove to the hospital, and sang carols to people who were stuck there on Christmas Day.

You might say, "Well, that's not much of a sacrifice. It was only a couple of hours." That's true, but it was a significant moment in the lives of our kids. Sacrifice means different things at different times in a person's life. Our kids saw our Christmas hospital trip as a major sacrifice. They wanted to play with their new toys, but they gave up that opportunity to go make Christmas memorable for others. Since that day, they have been open to other suggestions to sacrifice for others. And someday, God will undoubtedly call them to a deeper, more significant sacrifice.

Some of us conclude, "Sacrifice is just too hard." Do we think it was any easier for God? He gave us the greatest sacrifice of all time when He sent His Son into a dangerous world, not just at the risk of being misunderstood and rejected, but knowing He would be brutally killed.

God willingly gave His Son for us. That's sacrifice.

How would your life be different if you and your family lived this principle every day? What kind of impact would you have—on each other and on people in need? What kind of legacy would you leave to your kids?

It Starts with You

Your parents may have been great examples of the principles outlined in this chapter. If so, you have a wonderful heritage to pass along to your children. But some of you are on the other end of the stick. Your parents were terrible examples, and you're doing your best to learn from scratch how to teach your kids about money. Most of us are somewhere in the middle. Our parents modeled a few of the principles, but there are some holes in what we internalized when we were kids. Now we have the responsibility of learning these lessons for ourselves, and we have the solemn responsibility to pass them along to our children.

Of the eleven principles, pick one or two to focus on at first. Practice those for a few weeks or a month, until they become a habit for you. You'll probably encounter resistance, in your own mind and from your family. Don't be surprised, and don't quit! Keep learning and keep being the best example you can be for your kids.

In His greatest sermon, Jesus told His followers,

Don't store up treasures here on earth, where moths eat them and rust destroys them, and where thieves break in and steal. Store your treasures in heaven, where moths and rust cannot destroy, and thieves do not break in and steal. Wherever your treasure is, there the desires of your heart will also be. (Matt. 6:19–21)

None of the principles in this chapter is meant to be applied in a vacuum. We learn to value the right things only when we're amazed that God has put unlimited value on us. When we know we're His treasures, we put *our* treasures in the right places. First and foremost, He'll become our greatest treasure. We'll see ourselves as grateful recipients and as stewards entrusted with resources to use for His glory. When our kids see our hearts for God and for others, they'll want to make their lives count, too.

Chapter 9

How to Talk to Your Kids About Bullying

My friend Josh Clinton told about a painful experience from his school days:

It was a day just like any other day in junior high school. I was in the lunchroom eating my meal—that day it happened to be chili. (You'll soon see why that detail is important.) Unfortunately, the friends I usually sat with at lunch were on a field trip, so I had to sit alone.

I wasn't alone for long. Before I knew it, a boy named Kevin was standing behind me. He was an obnoxious guy who delighted in picking on people. He always said the most awful things and relentlessly teased the people he viewed as "easy targets." Since I was alone that day, he saw his opportunity.

He mocked me with a whine, "Ohhhh, poor Josh! The little baby's friends are all gone."

I tried to ignore Kevin's verbal jab and continued to eat lunch. I began to eat even faster so I could get out of the lunchroom and avoid anything worse—but I wasn't fast enough.

Kevin spoke loudly so others could hear his sneer, "He's sitting by himself because nobody else wants to sit by him!"

His words stung! In my heart, I knew they weren't true . . . or were they? Was I really a loser nobody wanted to sit by?

The more I ignored Kevin, the louder he talked. It seemed like everyone in the lunchroom was watching the drama unfold. I was nervous, scared, and hurt. Still, I tried to act like I was completely ignoring Kevin. I hoped he would lose interest and walk away. It didn't happen.

The next thing I knew, Kevin took a bowl of chili and poured it over my head! All of the kids who were watching began to laugh. They pointed and giggled at the guy who was dripping with chili.

I couldn't believe what had just happened. I had seen things like this in movies, but I was convinced no one could really be that cruel in real life. Who would pour an entire bowl of chili on top of someone's head in front of everyone in the lunchroom? But here I was . . . living out my very own Hollywood horror story.

One of the teachers came over to see what was happening. She barked, "What's going on here? How did this happen?"

Kevin immediately replied, "I tripped. It was just an accident."

I knew it was no accident, but I kept quiet. I was afraid of the repercussions if I told the teacher what really happened.

I went to the bathroom, washed my hair as best I could, and tried to make it through the rest of the day. I made it all the way through my classes without another incident, but when I got on the bus it started all over again.

One of Kevin's friends, Danny, had seen what had happened in the lunchroom, and he picked up right where Kevin left off.

Danny began to verbally torture me. He even began to talk about my mom. He said, "Hey Josh! How long is your mom's moustache?"

I'm not sure why that bothered me so much. My mother certainly didn't have a moustache, but Danny's slur still hurt me and made me angry. Rather than ignore him, I turned around, bumped him with my backpack, and told him to stop. Danny punched me in the mouth. I was wearing braces at the time, and the inside of my lips were cut and bleeding. I got off the bus as soon as I could.

I felt humiliated, defeated, and very, very small. I dreaded going to school the next day . . . and the next . . . and the next . . .

It's Not Funny

Bullying is a form of abuse[29] that's much more serious than common gossip, being ignored, or being called a name. Bullying is not funny. It causes real harm. According to the U.S. Department of Health and Human Services:

Bullying is unwanted, aggressive behavior among school aged children that involves a real or perceived power imbalance. The behavior is repeated, or has the potential to be repeated, over time. Bullying includes actions such as making threats, spreading rumors, attacking someone physically or verbally, and excluding someone from a group on purpose.[30]

The statistics about bullying are alarming:

- Nearly one-third of kids in grades six through ten are affected.

- About eight out of ten kids have reported being harassed.

- Six out of ten teenagers observe the impact of bullying at school at least once a day.

- Anxiety over being bullied causes 160,000 kids to miss school every year.

- Thirty-five percent of children have been the victims of cyberbullying.

- Bullies don't stop their behavior on the last day of school. Forty percent of boys who were bullies in grades six through nine had three or more arrests by the time they were thirty years old.

- Sixty-four percent of children who were bullied didn't report their experience.

- Seventy percent of students believe their schools have inadequate responses to bullying.[31]

All of these are only statistics, empty numbers, until our children become the victims of a bully. I'll never forget the night Jordan told Cherith and me about a boy who was bullying him at school. He was in the fourth grade. The boy, we'll call him Edward, had been pushing Jordan, making fun of him during the recess football games, and trying to exclude Jordan from his group of friends.

It all came to a head the day the boy tried to cut in line in front of Jordan. When Jordan said, "Hey, no cutting!" the boy turned around, picked Jordan up, and threw him over a desk and into a wall. Jordan's head smacked against the concrete wall, leaving him stunned and dizzy.

When he told us what happened, I was furious, but I knew I needed to handle this situation in an appropriate way. Cherith and I followed the pattern we recommend to parents who are trying to help their children cope with bullies.

When Your Child is a Victim . . .

1. Remind him he's not alone.

The victim of a bully usually feels isolated and abandoned. The child often shuts down emotionally and stuffs the hurt, fear, and anger rather than report the incident.

If you notice your child withdrawing or reacting disproportionately to everyday events, ask some questions about what's going on at school. It may take some time for your child to open up, but be patient.

If you notice your child withdrawing or reacting disproportionately to everyday events, ask some questions about what's going on at school.

Before Jordan told us about the bullying incident, Cherith noticed him being uncharacteristically anxious. In fact, all weekend he had looked nervous, and he complained of headaches and difficulty breathing. On the way home from church Sunday night, Cherith realized Jordan was having what seemed like a panic attack in the back seat.

"What's wrong, buddy?" she asked.

At first he was reluctant to talk, but Cherith gently asked some loving questions. Eventually, Jordan told us the entire story of the incident with Edward and the problems leading up to it.

If you discover your child is the victim of a bully, remind him that you're going to walk with him through this ordeal. He isn't alone.

In most cases, the bully has other victims, too. Jordan told us the reason he had been taking all of the abuse from Edward was because he knew that if Edward wasn't picking on him, he would be targeting other boys in the class. Jordan figured he was doing those other boys a favor by letting Edward focus on him. Jordan said, "I figured every minute he spent picking on me was one minute he wasn't picking on them."

Cherith and I explained that while it was noble of him to take the other boys' punishment, it was more important that he take steps to get the bullying stopped altogether so that neither he nor the other boys would ever have to endure Edward's abuse again.

2. Tell your child the bullying is not her problem.

Communicate to your child that she didn't provoke the bully's actions. Many children assume they're deficient or flawed in some way, and that makes the bullying justified. Assure your child that's not the case. No one but the bully is responsible for his or her behavior.

Bullying is another case where "hurt people hurt people." Bullies are usually hurting and insecure, and inflicting pain is the way they try to dominate others. They feel out of control, so they attempt to control other people by attacking, teasing, and intimidating. They may witness this kind of behavior at home, or they may feel abandoned and lash out in anger at anyone who seems vulnerable. None of those reasons excuses their behavior. It's important to remember that the bully has the problem, not the victim.

3. Don't suggest that your child "just ignore it."

A lot of parents tell their kids, "If you ignore the person, he'll stop. He's just looking for a reaction from you." That's not always true. By failing to respond with strength and truth, the child becomes even more vulnerable and sets himself up for future torture. Many times ignoring the problem unwittingly gives the bully a sense of power, escalating the abuse.

4. Encourage your child to tell those in authority about the bullying.

Your first instinct will be to defend your child. (I know mine was.) You want to go straight to the school, or church, or wherever the bullying is happening, and wring that kid's neck! Resist that urge. Instead, foster your child's autonomy. Give him power and authority to take action. He should tell the teacher or principal so that he learns to communicate with adults about serious problems. Of course, coach your child about what to say, and role-play the conversation. If necessary, you can accompany your child, but let him speak as much as possible. Be supportive, but don't get in the way.

A recent study of children ages nine to thirteen showed: "Half the respondents said they have been bullied at least once in a while. When bullied, almost half said they fight back, about a fourth tell an adult, and twenty percent do nothing; only eight percent try to talk to the bully. Nearly two-thirds claimed they tell or try to stop bullying when they see it, but sixteen percent do nothing, and twenty percent join in."[32]

Make sure your child knows someone she can talk to, whether it's you, a school counselor, a teacher, or a pastor. Resist the immediate temptation to handle the situation on your own by going to the school and talking to the principal yourself. This strategy may backfire. Often, word gets back to the bully and gives him more ammo. He can say, "Your mommy came and told on me," and the bullying gets worse. By allowing your child to speak up and handle the bullying on her own, you're empowering her and involving her in the solution.

Give the proper authorities several chances to address the problem. They may be overwhelmed with other responsibilities, and they may not give enough attention to your child's problem until you become a squeaky wheel. It may require several conversations, the first few initiated by your child, and eventually your involvement. If the people in authority fail to respond, or they respond and nothing changes, go to a higher authority and ask for help.

5. Don't accept lame excuses.

When bullies are cornered, they look for an easy way out. No matter how badly they've hurt someone, they insist, "Hey, I was only kidding!" "I didn't mean any harm." Or, "Oh, that didn't hurt anybody. What's the big deal?"

Expect this kind of excuse, but don't buy it. Don't let your child buy it either. Try to use this painful experience to open the door for some insightful conversations between you and your child about the nature of the human heart. Your child might become a bit more observant, a bit shrewder, and a bit wiser about who can be trusted. Those are wonderful traits that most of us don't learn until we have to. Being the victim of a bully is a time when they have to!

> **Try to use this painful experience to open the door for some insightful conversations between you and your child about the nature of the human heart.**

6. If the bullying doesn't stop after the authorities are involved, speak to the other child's parents directly.

If nothing changes after several attempts to convince the responsible authorities to take action, it may be time for you to talk to the bully's parents—not the bully, the bully's parents. Assume the best of the other parents and set up a meeting or a lengthy phone call to talk about the situation. Don't attack, and don't express too much emotion. State your confidence that they want their child to act responsibly. Instead of accusing, review the facts and ask for the parents' help in solving the problem. Most people are far more agreeable when they believe you want to be on their side. In fact, ask them how *they* want to handle the situation.

If the mom agrees to rein in her unruly child, thank her and say, "I hope you'll call me if my child bothers anyone." If the bullying persists, call her back and ask for her help again. It won't take long before she realizes you aren't going to put up with her child's behavior.

If the parent is resistant and accuses you of overprotecting your child, you can say, "I can tell that we see this very differently. I'm not asking for your child to become my child's best friend. I'm only asking you for some help to make life better for all of us." If the bullying persists, call the parent back and begin the process again. Sooner or later, your tenacity will probably convince the parent to step in and take action. Throughout it all, remain calm and fact-centered.

7. Remind your child that he has the right to defend himself.

You never want to encourage retaliation or revenge, but make sure your child knows that you completely approve of using physical force for self-protection. You can say, "If someone is hurting you, do whatever you need to do to get away from the bully and find a safe place."

Some Christians believe they and their kids should always "turn the other cheek," but this is often misunderstood. It means we don't take revenge, but it doesn't mean we don't protect ourselves. Jesus didn't let the Pharisees bully Him during His ministry. He often defended Himself. (Look at the escalating confrontation in John 6!) At times He slipped away from confrontations when it was appropriate. Only at the end, when He was prepared to make His complete sacrifice for us, did He let Himself be mocked, tortured, and killed. Even then, when a guard struck Him, Jesus protested that the blow was illegal (John 18:22–23).

Paul had more than his share of physical attacks and abuse. He was as tough as nails, yet when he was threatened, he appealed to the Romans for protection. When the Roman courts failed to protect his rights, he appealed to Caesar himself. In his final letter, he warned Timothy about a bully: "Alexander the coppersmith did me much harm, but the Lord will judge him for what he has done. Be careful of him, for he fought against everything we said" (2 Tim. 4:14–15).

In counseling a child to respond to a bully, parents often move to one extreme or the other—and often they disagree on which extreme to pursue. One insists, "Jesus wants you to turn the other cheek, so you need to take whatever the bully does to you." The other parent growls, "Never take that kind of treatment! Fight back!"

We can advise our kids to defend themselves for two reasons: for self-protection and for the bully's good.

Consider a different approach. We can advise our kids to defend themselves for two reasons: for self-protection and for the bully's good. Letting a bully continue to harm others isn't a loving way to treat him or her. Love demands inter-vention—strong, honest, loving intervention that gives the bully an opportunity to change.

8. Pray for courage

David faced a giant bully, Goliath, but he knew he wasn't facing him on his own. He prayed to God for courage to face his enemy. He declared that the battle was not his, but God's.

Before he went into battle, David told the bully:

> "You come to me with sword, spear, and javelin, but I come to you in the name of the Lord of Heaven's Armies—the God of the armies of Israel, whom you have defied. Today the Lord will conquer you, and I will kill you and cut off your head. And then I will give the dead bodies of your men to the birds and wild animals, and the whole world will know that there is a God in Israel! And every-one assembled here will know that the Lord rescues his people, but not with sword and spear. This is the Lord's battle, and he will give you to us!" (1 Sam. 17:45–47)

Now that's standing up to a bully in the power of the Spirit!

9. Love and pray for the bully.

It may seem crazy, especially when we're the victims of abuse, but Jesus challenges us to "Love your enemies! Pray for those who persecute you!" (Matt. 5:44)

Loving a bully doesn't mean we let him continue in his abusive behavior, just like loving an alcoholic doesn't mean we make excuses for his lies and irresponsible behavior. Love requires more than passivity. It demands involvement, firmly speaking the truth, and stopping him from sinning, at least against us.

Loving a bully also involves praying that God will reveal Himself, show the bully the damage he's doing, and give him the willingness to stop. We can also ask God to heal the hurts that are driving the bully's behavior.

10. Communicate a long-term perspective.

When kids are bullied, they dread every moment of every day. They live in fear that the next moment, the next class period, or the next encounter in the hall will bring the verbal and physical attacks they dread. As you help your kids apply all the principles we've already outlined, assure them of one more truth: Someday they will reap the benefits of the lessons they're learning about being strong in the face of adversity, but if the bullies don't change, they will almost certainly suffer a tragic life of broken relationships, distrust, and emptiness.

A friend got a glimpse of the future, and it helped her understand what God had done in her life:

> I was bullied terribly in middle school. Those were the worst years of my life. I came home crying every day

because more popular kids picked on me. I told my mom about it. She talked to my teachers, but nothing was ever really done. They kept saying mean things to me and snickering behind my back. My mom told me that someday these kids would be a distant memory. One day I would be successful, and they would all be miserable. She said I would meet real friends and have them forever. I wanted to believe her. I hoped she was right.

Later in school I entered a wonderful new reality. I made real friends—people I trusted and who trusted me. During that time, I met my college roommate and my maid of honor.

Now that I have graduated from college and have my own family, I occasionally hear stories about the people who bullied me years ago. Almost all of them have messed up their lives and are struggling terribly. Thankfully, God has given me the ability to forgive them, so I don't rejoice when I hear bad news about them. In fact, I pray for them.

Without my student ministry at church, that would never have happened. That's why I go above and beyond to help my stepchildren get plugged in at church with other kids and make real friends. I've encouraged my kids to not only forgive those who bully them, but to stand up to them and pray for them. Together, we can trust God to help us through it.

11. *Follow up with your child by asking questions.*

After your child has been bullied and you have taken steps to resolve the problem, don't just say, "How was your day?" Be more specific:

- "Did you see the bully today?"

- "Did she talk to you?"

- "Did he do anything inappropriate?"

- "How did you respond?"

- "How did she then respond to you?"

After each question, listen carefully. Your child may want to talk about what happened that day, or he may not. If he didn't respond with strength to the bully, his pain may be blended with shame. Remember that the goal isn't just to stop the bully, but to teach your child the skills to respond with wisdom and strength for the rest of his life. This goal is much bigger and more lasting, and it requires ongoing teaching and coaching rather than emotional outbursts, demands for control or revenge, or attempts to deny the situation and the pain.

12. Widen the circle of support.

When a child is bullied, she needs all the help she can get. Consider asking grandparents or other extended family members to provide plenty of love and encouragement. Make it clear that you don't want the other person(s) to take over, and you don't want unsolicited advice because it may be different from yours. Take time to coach the family member(s) and make sure it's a team effort to provide the care your child needs at this difficult time.

13. Watch what's happening online.

Cyberbullying is a recent, but now common phenomenon. Aggressive, attacking behavior is no longer reserved for the lunchroom or playground. Kids have access to a wide array of social media, and with those connections cyberbullying has become a problem twenty-four hours a day, seven days a week. With a single click, hostility, lies, and innuendoes can spread instantly to thousands of people.

Opening the Door

Encounters with bullies usually end well only if the young victims are adequately coached to handle the crisis. Authors Lee Hirsch and Cynthia Lowen offer their advice in *Bully: An Action Plan for Teachers, Parents, and Communities to Combat the Bullying Crisis*:

> Parents are absolutely critical for spreading values of empathy, of kindness, of not perpetrating violence or

supporting violence in their own home. Even if you bring up the subject with your kids, don't expect them to come right out and tell you if they're being bullied. [33]

Hirsch and Lowen observe that parents are often the last to find out about the problem. Their kids are embarrassed, afraid of how their parents will react, and terrified they'll receive even harsher treatment if they speak up. They may also conclude that the way the bully is treating them is completely normal.

The authors suggest asking indirect questions that are less threatening to the child, such as:

- "What kinds of cliques are there at your school?"

- "Do you have someone to sit with at lunch or on the bus?"

- "Do you feel like there are a lot of rumors about you going around?"

Let me go back to the situation between Jordan and Edward. After we talked with Jordan about Edward's behavior, he took the initiative to tell his teacher. The teacher confronted Edward, and the bullying stopped. The two never became good friends, but the following year they met on the playground and Edward said, "You're a pretty cool guy, Jordan." That comment made Jordan feel ten feet tall. He knew he had handled it the right way.

Of course, encounters with bullies don't always turn out so well. We can't determine the bully's response. All we can control is our communication with our children. Our goal is to provide support, affirmation, a clear path forward, and the skills needed to walk that path. If the child learns these lessons, we've helped him handle difficult relationships for the rest of his life. That's not a bad outcome at all.

Chapter 10

How to Talk to Your Kids About Restoring Broken Relationships

His name was Wayne. I'll never forget his name, and I'll never forget his face. We met in high school, and we quickly became friends. We hung out together all the time. As we approached graduation, Wayne decided to go to the same college where I had been accepted.

Until that point, I had put up with a particularly annoying aspect of our friendship: Wayne was jealous whenever

I spent time with anyone else. He didn't just want to be a friend, even a good friend. He wanted to be my *only* friend. I tried many times to make it clear that I wanted to have a lot of friends, but for some strange reason, none of my explanations mattered. You can call it codependency, a smothering relationship, or just plain weird, but Wayne was fixated on me—not sexually, but emotionally.

One day during our sophomore year of college, he snapped. He was angry because I had chosen to be roommates with someone else the next semester. I mean he flipped out—emotionally, and totally! He decided if he wasn't going to be my best friend, he would be my worst enemy.

From that moment, when I saw him on campus he walked past me like he didn't even know me. I always said, "Hey, Wayne," but he ignored me. That was strange enough, but it didn't end there. Wayne was out for blood. He began trashing me to everyone on campus—and he had plenty of ammo. Since he had been a close friend for several years, he knew a lot of embarrassing things about me. (Hey, don't judge. We were all idiots in high school!) He decided to share every gory detail with anyone who would listen.

Suddenly, people I hardly knew—and some I'd never met—began to stop me and ask about things they had heard about me. Most of the things were dumb mistakes I'd made three or four years earlier, but they were true . . . or at least, true enough that I couldn't deny them. The strangers who stopped me didn't know whether to laugh with me or console me.

Wayne ruined my reputation, and he loved it. Sometimes I saw him smiling in the distance as people stopped to talk to me, but soon my past embarrassments became too mundane for him. To make his stories more dramatic, he created additional "facts" that were completely untrue.

Had I done anything to deserve this? Not at all. I had been patient, kind, and friendly with him during all those years. Did I want to strangle him? Absolutely! On more than one occasion, I came very close to giving him the "right hand of fellowship"!

My time in college should have been a wonderful experience, but those were hard years. Wayne's misguided vengeance poisoned them. After graduation we lost touch with each other, but I didn't lose touch with the impact of Wayne's actions. The wounds went deep, and I thought about him a lot. I struggled for years with a desire to inflict the same pain on him that he inflicted on me—or worse. The painful memories simply wouldn't fade. Almost any painful event immediately took me back to the many times Wayne had maliciously and intentionally slandered me.

Deep Wounds

How about you? Has there been a Wayne in your life? Has anyone inflicted pain and caused you heartache? Maybe a friend abandoned you and continues to spread lies about you. Perhaps a passive-aggressive ex-spouse chooses to lash out and make things difficult for you, even though you're not married anymore. Maybe someone at work has targeted you because you have a position he wants, and he's committed to destroy you to get it. Perhaps a family member carries a longstanding grudge and makes every family get-together a battle zone.

The hurt can go even deeper. Some of us live each day with the nagging, open wounds of emotional, physical, and sexual hurts caused by those who should have been our closest allies and protectors: our parents. Beth told her story of deep pain:

> Living a life of abuse gives you plenty of reasons to hurt. One of mine is the pain of a lost childhood: I've always had to be a grownup, even when I was ten. I suffered excruciating pain from a dad who blurred the line about what a healthy sex life looks like. He crossed the lines. He sexually abused me at night and physically abused my siblings during the day.

> It took me a while to understand why I was just as angry with my mother. I realized she could and should have stepped in to protect me, but she didn't. She cared more about avoiding conflict with my dad than caring for me in my darkest moments. Actually, this pain is even harder to bear. Really, how did she not miss him when he got

out of bed for long periods each night? How could she not see or hear what was happening to my siblings and me? She knew; she just didn't care enough.

Chances are, you have a name or a face in your mind right now, someone who has hurt you, maybe without provocation. That person has caused you intense heartache, and the wounds have clouded every subsequent relationship and endeavor in your life.

Unnatural but Necessary

Author Philip Yancey has called forgiveness "the unnatural act" because everything in us screams for revenge when we've been hurt.[34] People may respond to this vengeful urge in very different ways: some actively plot ways to harm the one who hurt them; some use more subtle, passive-aggressive means (such as gossip) to inflict pain; and others stuff their powerful, painful feelings inside, hoping the hurt will go away. All victims of harm instinctively realize that the way God created the world to work has gone wrong . . . terribly wrong.

God has given all of us an innate sense of justice. We believe offenders should be stopped and perpetrators should be punished. He assures us they will be, but the problem is that we assume *we* should be the agents of justice. That's called revenge.

Revenge should be left to God. Our challenge is to try to forgive. Forgiveness can be explained and understood in several very important ways:

- When others sin against us, they create a debt. Forgiveness means *we* pay the debt instead of insisting *they* pay it.

- When we pay the debt, we choose not to inflict pain through revenge. Instead, we grieve the loss we've suffered until the pain subsides.

> **Revenge should be left to God.**
> **Our challenge is to try to forgive.**

- We long for justice, and we trust that God will ultimately be just. We can count on Him to deal with the person instead of insisting on taking revenge to enact our own version of justice.

- Forgiveness is a point and a process. We choose to forgive someone at a point in time, but the hurt and anger linger until we've gone through the grief process.

- We can't give away what we don't possess. Our ability and power to forgive is motivated only by acknowledgment of and gratitude for the forgiveness we have received for our own sins.

- Grudges tend to linger. One sign that we still have some work to do in forgiving someone is that we enjoy hearing bad news about that person.

- We can teach our kids how to forgive only to the extent we have learned how to forgive those who have hurt us.

Ironically, Christians often have great difficulty forgiving others. Why? Because they assume their intense feelings of hurt and anger are so wrong—so ungodly—that they need to do anything and everything to get rid of them immediately. But none of their shortcuts work. They try to tell themselves the offense wasn't that bad (minimizing), or the other person didn't mean to hurt them (excusing), or the event didn't happen at all (denial). Pastor and author Lewis Smedes has a different recommendation: "When we forgive evil we do not excuse it, we do not tolerate it, we do not smother it. We look the evil full in the face, call it what it is, let its horror shock and stun and enrage us, and only then do we forgive it."[35]

The Poison of Unforgiveness

Your children are watching you. In fact they've been watching you, their grandparents, and every other member of the family to see how each of you responds to offenses—from inside the family and from without. If you minimize, excuse, or deny the hurt inflicted by someone else, they'll copy those faulty coping mechanisms. When you don't forgive, the hurt soon festers into the poisons of self-pity and an entrenched identity as a victim. The problem is that this new identity feels so right!

Pastor Frederick Buechner describes the impact of refusing to forgive:

> Of the Seven Deadly Sins, anger is possibly the most fun. To lick your wounds, to smack your lips over grievances long past, to roll over your tongue the prospect of bitter confrontations still to come, to savor to the last toothsome morsel both the pain you are given and the pain you are giving back—in many ways it is a feast fit for a king. The chief drawback is that what you are wolfing down is yourself. The skeleton at the feast is you![36]

When we choose not to forgive and instead hold on to the hurt, we cause more damage to ourselves than to the one who hurt us. We long for justice, but we insist on somehow becoming the prosecutor, judge, jury, and executioner. That person should pay, we're convinced, and we're going to be sure it happens!

We become like the little boy who was sitting on a park bench in obvious, intense pain. A man walking by asked him what was wrong. The boy said, "I'm sitting on a bee."

The man asked, "Then why don't you get up?"

The boy answered, "Because I figure I'm hurting him more than he's hurting me!"

This story may sound silly, but countless people are like the little boy. We can't stop thinking about the person who hurt us, and we can't stop thinking about ways to get even. We keep people locked up in the dungeon of our minds, hoping that our negative thoughts will somehow make us feel better. They won't. They can't. We're not hurting the other person at all by being consumed with thoughts of the offense and revenge. The truth is that we're only hurting ourselves.

God will heal our wounds when we get up off the park bench—when we stop mentally holding captive the people who have hurt us. If we don't allow God to heal our wounds from the past, the hurts will turn to hate, the hate will turn to bitterness, and bitterness inevitably leads to loneliness. We need to ask God to heal us and give us the power to forgive.

Unpacking the Backpack

No matter what the offense might be, you have a choice: to forgive, grieve, and heal . . . or to harbor a grudge. When you choose to hold a grudge, you keep, entertain, and even cherish the hard feelings you have toward the person who hurt you. It doesn't matter how many weeks, months, or years go by, you stay angry with the person. You spread gossip to slander him. If you hear he is suffering, you're glad, and it disgusts you if he's successful. You can't look the person in the eye, and you can't think of anything nice to say—to him or about him.

Holding grudges is like carrying a backpack full of rocks. At first, our ungrieved losses and unhealed hurts are a few big rocks in the backpack—bad enough, but bearable. Yet as time goes on, every refusal to forgive and every thought about getting even adds another rock. Before long, the weight of the backpack makes life difficult. The more we struggle, the more we blame the offender. We tell our friends, "Look what she did to me!" Every aspect of our lives is affected: relationships, goals, spiritual life, and even physical health crumble under the strain.

All the while, the offender doesn't know or care how we feel. Our grudge is killing us, but it's not affecting the other person at all. We're robbing ourselves of the joy God can provide. That's dumb, really dumb.

> ### The solution—for us and for our kids when people hurt them—is to learn the restorative art and skill of forgiveness.

The solution—for us and for our kids when people hurt them—is to learn the restorative art and skill of forgiveness. Lewis Smedes reminds us: "Vengeance is having a videotape planted in your soul that cannot be turned off. It plays the painful scene over and over again inside your mind. . . . And each time it plays you feel the clap of pain again.... Forgiving turns off the videotape of pained memory. Forgiving sets you free."[37]

The Power Source

In Paul's letter to the Colossians, he explained the vital connection between experiencing God's forgiveness and the ability to forgive others: "Since God chose you to be the holy people he loves, you must clothe yourselves with tenderhearted mercy, kindness, humility, gentleness, and patience. Make allowance for each other's faults, and forgive anyone who offends you. Remember, the Lord forgave you, so you must forgive others" (Col. 3:12–13).

We can only express forgiveness to those who have sinned against us *to the extent* we have experienced the love, acceptance, and forgiveness of Christ. When we're tempted to harbor a grudge, we need to remember that Jesus didn't harbor one against us. He forgave. He paid the debt we couldn't pay, suffered the pain we should have suffered, and offered us a restored relationship with Him. Our experience of the vast sea of God's amazing grace should give us the resources to forgive those who have hurt us.

God willingly forgives every one of us when we sin against Him. He never holds a grudge, and He never takes revenge. If we're going to live the life God has planned for us, we need to follow His example. We must forgive every person of every wrong. It's not easy, but with God's help, we can do it!

People might say, "I don't know how to forgive. It's too hard. I have way too much anger, and the pain is far too deep. Besides, you don't know what he did to me. It was bad, really bad. You don't know how much he hurt me!"

Paul gives us an important insight into forgiveness in his letter to the Romans. He wrote:

Never pay back evil with more evil. Do things in such a way that everyone can see you are honorable. Do all that you can to live in peace with everyone. Dear friends, never take revenge. Leave that to the righteous anger of God. For the Scriptures say,

"I will take revenge;
I will pay them back,"
says the Lord.

Instead,

"If your enemies are hungry, feed them.
If they are thirsty, give them something to drink.
In doing this, you will heap
burning coals of shame on their heads."

Don't let evil conquer you, but conquer evil by doing good (Rom. 12:17–21).

Paul is teaching us that when we forgive, we're choosing to take the offenders off our hook, and we put them on God's hook. We no longer insist on taking revenge; instead, we trust Him to be righteous and just with the persons. If we have confidence in His justice, we can forgive.

As we've seen, this doesn't mean our intense feelings will immediately turn to warmth and affection. We still have to grieve and heal, which takes time. But every time those thoughts of revenge or feelings of hurt come up again, we can remind ourselves that we've put the person in God's hands. How many times do we need to remember this truth? As many as it takes.

Teaching Kids to Forgive

When talking to your kids about forgiveness, share the story of Joseph in the Old Testament. Joseph's brothers were jealous of him. Their father Jacob showed favoritism, treating Joseph better than he treated the other sons, so they hatched a plan to get rid of him. They threw Joseph in a pit. When some traders were passing by on their way to Egypt, they changed their plans and sold him into slavery.

Joseph became the slave of a royal official whose wife tried to seduce him. When he refused, she falsely accused Joseph of sexual assault. He was thrown into prison, where he languished for many years. When the pharaoh had disturbing dreams, Joseph was able to interpret them. Joseph

told him that seven years of abundant harvest would be followed by seven years of famine. His interpretations were
true and accurate, and the pharaoh was impressed. He
made Joseph the second in command of the entire nation of
Egypt! Joseph's job was to manage the inventory of grain so
that everyone could survive the seven lean years.

The famine struck the entire region, including the area
where Joseph's father, Jacob, and his other brothers lived.
The brothers went to Egypt to buy grain so they could survive. When they arrived, they didn't recognize their brother,
and he didn't tell them who he was. Joseph tested them in
several ways to see if they had changed, and when he was
satisfied they had been humbled and could be trusted, he
revealed his identity.

During all those years, Joseph could have wallowed in
bitterness and self-pity, but he chose to trust God. The Lord
gave him insight into the situation. When their father died,
the brothers thought Joseph might finally take revenge.
Fearing for their lives, they offered to become his slaves!
Joseph explained his God-given insight to his brothers:

> "Don't be afraid of me. Am I God, that I can punish you?
> You intended to harm me, but God intended it all for
> good. He brought me to this position so I could save the
> lives of many people. No, don't be afraid. I will continue
> to take care of you and your children." (Gen. 50:19–21)

Even though his brothers' actions had been blatantly evil and had cost him many years of slavery and prison, Joseph saw that God had a purpose even for his suffering. Joseph didn't forgive his brothers at the moment he had them in his power; he had forgiven them *long before* they showed up in Egypt looking for food.

From Joseph, we learn some lessons about forgiveness—what it's not and what it is.

> ## Joseph didn't forgive his brothers at the moment he had them in his power; he had forgiven them *long before* they showed up in Egypt looking for food.

Forgiveness is not pretending that nothing happened.

When his brothers showed up, Joseph didn't say, "Hey, I'm your brother, Joseph. Let's go have some pizza." He didn't minimize their sins against him, he didn't say it wasn't their fault, and he didn't act like nothing ever happened. He told them plainly, "You intended harm." Moreover, he didn't trust them until they had proven they had changed and were now trustworthy.

Some people think forgiveness is pretending the offender didn't hurt them, but that confuses everyone—both the sinner and the one sinned against. If we act as if nothing happened, we don't forgive, and bitterness grows.

304 TALK NOW AND LATER

Forgiveness isn't taking the blame for the other person's sin.

Joseph didn't say, "Hey guys, I know you sold me into slavery, but it was really my fault. I was such a bad brother. I never should have worn the colorful robe Dad gave me. I probably would have sold me into slavery, too. It's all my fault."

Some people blame everyone and everything, but they never take responsibility for their sins. Just as bad is the opposite response: the victim's attempt to resolve conflict and get rid of hurtful emotions by taking the blame when not at fault at all. Those two reactions often occur in the same household!

Admit it when you've done wrong, but don't take the blame for someone else's offense. If you give people an excuse for abusing or controlling you, they will take it. Subsequently, they'll never learn to be honest, to be responsible, and to confess their sins.

Forgiveness includes blessing those who hurt us.

As the second most powerful man in Egypt, Joseph could have had his brothers killed in an instant, or he could have refused to let them have any grain and they would have starved to death. But Joseph didn't try to harm them. Even while testing them, he gave them grain so their families could survive. Then, when they passed the test of trustworthiness, Joseph invited his father and everyone in the family to move to a lush and fertile section of Egypt.

If Joseph had harbored a grudge, he would have used all those opportunities to hurt his brothers, but instead, he blessed them. That's the fruit of genuine forgiveness—blessing instead of cursing.

Before we can bless those who have hurt us, we have to dig deep into the love of God.

Again, everything in us wants justice, or rather, revenge. Before we can bless those who have hurt us, we have to dig deep into the love of God. We were sinners, enemies of God. We deserved only His wrath and judgment, but instead God gave us the greatest blessing imaginable: Himself and His grace. And every time we sin, God reminds us that He has already paid the price through Christ's sacrifice for us. We don't deserve God's love and forgiveness, but He "lavishes" it on us anyway. When we're convinced that God blesses us even though we're sinners, we will be able to bless those who have sinned against us.

We can follow Joseph's example. He forgave his brothers, blessed them, and never brought up their offense again. How could he forgive like that? I think it's because he also knew the truth that Paul would later teach: "Remember, the Lord forgave you, so you must forgive others" (Col. 3:13).

Forgiveness lets us hold the person accountable, but without manipulation.

A misconception of forgiveness is that we no longer hold the person accountable for her sinful, harmful actions. Yes, forgiveness means that we absorb the debt instead of inflicting pain in vengeance on the offending person, but love requires us to then seek the best for her, which includes holding her accountable. The first step, though, is to forgive. Only then will we hold people accountable for the right reasons.

In *The Reason for God*, pastor and author Tim Keller explains the progression and the purpose of holding people accountable:

> When I counsel forgiveness to people who have been harmed, they often ask about the wrongdoers, "Shouldn't they be held accountable?" I usually respond, "Yes, but only if you forgive them." There are many good reasons that we should want to confront wrongdoers. We should confront wrongdoers to wake them up to their real character, to move them to repair their relationships, or to at least constrain them and protect others from being harmed by them in the future. Notice, however, that all those reasons for confrontation are reasons of love. The best way to love them and the other potential victims around them is to confront them in the hope they will repent, change, and make things right. The desire for vengeance, however, is motivated not by good will but by ill will.[38]

Forgiveness opens the door to reconciliation.

Many people are confused about the relationship of forgiveness and reconciliation. One man told me, "I'm not going to forgive my dad because if I forgive, I'll have to trust him—and he's not trustworthy!" That's a common misunderstanding.

Forgiveness is unilateral. We can forgive even if the offender never admits what he did was wrong. He may not be sorry or trustworthy, and he may never intend to change. Yet when we forgive, our hearts become free from the slavery of holding a grudge.

However, reconciliation requires both parties to be trustworthy. For reconciliation to take place, we choose to forgive, and we open the door to the *possibility* of a restored relationship. The relationship can only be restored if several things happen: the other person must admit what he did was wrong; he must express genuine sorrow over the pain he caused; he must promise not to hurt us again; and he must make restitution for what was lost. Forgiveness can begin in an instant, but reconciliation is always a process. After trust has been shattered, it takes time to rebuild it—time to give the person plenty of opportunities to show he is trustworthy.

How long? We often make one of two mistakes: we trust too quickly, before seeing genuine change in the other person, or we refuse to trust even when the other person has proven he has changed.

When You Need to Be Forgiven

Of course, the problem isn't always *them*; sometimes it's *us*. We hurt people, we manipulate, we're selfish, and we ignore people who need us. When we've sinned against someone, we often try to use the same three methods to make it go away: minimizing ("It wasn't that bad"), excusing ("I couldn't help it"), or denial ("I don't know what you're talking about!").

As long as we put off confession—first to God and then to the other person—we live under a cloud of guilt. To get to the point of confession and repentance, we can follow a few important principles:

1. Don't avoid the person you've offended.

That's our natural inclination, isn't it? When we know we've hurt someone, we stay as far away as possible. We avoid eye contact, we keep our conversation superficial, and we leave as soon as we can. We dread being called out for what we've done, so we avoid the person, but that only makes the hurt worse.

Don't wait for the offended person to take the initiative. Take the first step. Usually, both parties are somewhat responsible, but don't wait. Jesus said, "If another believer sins against you, go privately and point out the offense. If the other person listens and confesses it, you have won that person back" (Matt. 18:15). But He also said, "Therefore, if you are offering your gift at the altar and there remember that your brother or sister has something against you, leave your gift there in front of the altar. First go and be reconciled to them; then come and offer your gift" (Matt. 5:23–24, NIV). So either way, whether we're the offended or the offender, Jesus tells us to take the initiative and attempt to resolve the conflict.

> ### Whether we're the offended or the offender, Jesus tells us to take the initiative and attempt to resolve the conflict.

2. Be honest with yourself about what you did and the depth of hurt you caused.

No matter how much it hurts to think of yourself as "a bad person," you'll never move toward wholeness until you're truthful about the seriousness of your mistake or sin. It hurts to be honest. We feel embarrassed and ashamed, but we need to remember that Jesus paid the ultimate price for us to be forgiven. Repentance shouldn't be *the last* thing we do; it should be *the first* thing because it reminds us of the love and grace of God! The experience of grace enables us to be honest because we're no longer afraid of condemnation. And besides, we'll never be honest with others if we can't first be honest with ourselves.

3. Confess your sins to the person you wronged.

What does a confession sound like? Three words: "I was wrong."

Don't wait for the person to come to you. When you know you've done wrong, go to the person and admit it. If at all possible, confession should be in person, face-to-face. You want her to not only hear your words but also to sense your heart. Seeing her reaction helps you know if you've convinced her you're sincere. If you can't go in person, talk on the phone. If you can't talk on the phone, write or email. Whatever your course of action, don't make excuses and don't delay. Do it as soon as possible.

4. Apologize.

An apology sounds like this: "I'm so sorry I hurt you."

In your apology, communicate genuine sorrow to the person you've wounded. Depending on the depth and frequency of the wound, he may not believe you. If you aren't visibly sorrowful and broken, he'll doubt you've truly come to grips with how deeply you've hurt him.

How can you tell if you feel sincere remorse? You can ask yourself: *Am I sorry for being caught, or am I sorry for the hurt I've caused? Have I cried about the wound I've inflicted and the loss I've caused? Can I put myself in the other person's shoes and feel what he feels?*

If you aren't brokenhearted, you may not have truly come to grips with how deeply you've hurt the other person.

Let me offer a word of caution: don't put on a "show of emotion." If you come across as phony, you'll only inflict another wound. The other person can sense when your emotion is sincere. Remember, he already doesn't trust you. If you attempt to mislead him about your emotional response to your offense, you'll only set the relationship back further.

5. Make restitution.

In many cases, the other person's loss is severe. Part of repentance is to make up for the loss. Often the payback is "in kind." If we stole money, we pay back the amount plus interest. If we broke something, we buy a new one. But sometimes we can't pay the person back in kind. We've broken the person's heart, and we can't mend that with money or things. We can, however, give intangibles of time, attention, kindness, and assistance.

If we don't offer to make restitution, the person who suffered the loss has every reason to wonder if our repentance is genuine.

Remember . . .

Pastor Rod Loy identifies three components to an effective apology:

"I was wrong." We might also say, "I make no excuses for what I did."

"I'm sorry." We might add, "It's my fault. It never should have happened."

"What can I do to make it right?" And prepare to do what they ask!

If you miss one of those three components, your apology isn't completely effective.

The Rest of Beth's Story

Earlier in this chapter Beth told her story of being sexually abused by her father and emotionally abandoned by her mother. Beth learned the lessons outlined in these pages. She explained,

I chose to forgive my parents, and with that decision, I had a lot of grieving and healing to do. God worked deeply to restore my heart. After a while, my pain was no longer the biggest thing in my vision each day. I thought about my children. I longed for them to have a relationship with my parents, their grandparents, but I was very cautious. If it was going to happen at all, it had to be in a controlled environment. When I thought about letting my parents spend time with my children, I had to process another layer of hurt and anger. I had to go deeper into forgiveness, which was a good thing. I also had to be crystal clear about who had been responsible for the abuse and neglect. I couldn't be cloudy about that. I had to genuinely forgive, not excuse.

As I forgave and assigned responsibility, I felt a new sense of freedom. Talk about liberating! Now when I take my kids to see my parents, I control every moment. My father was initially resistant, but soon he saw that his belligerence and demands weren't going to intimidate me anymore. If he wanted a relationship with his grandkids, he had to follow my rules. My rules are strict to protect my kids, but they are also full of grace.

For me, forgiving my parents was a choice at a point in time, and it continues to be a process. On every holiday—especially Christmas, Father's Day, Mother's Day, and birthdays—a wave of awful memories sweeps over me. Again, I have to choose to forgive them, or maybe, to remember that I've already forgiven them. I used to think I would someday "be over" all the pain, but it doesn't quite work that way. I still carry scars from the wounds I experienced, but scars aren't gaping wounds. They are signs of genuine healing.

Beth's healing process wasn't finished. She forgave her parents and offered a bridge to the future, but she also realized she had caused some deep wounds in her husband and children. She explained,

> As a spouse and parent, my pain spilled out in destructive and angry ways. I had the sharpest words and a harsh attitude all the time. It didn't take much for me to lash out. I was demanding, intimidating, and horrible. Every day around the house, my husband and children walked on eggshells. I was angry with everyone and about everything.
>
> My children lived in fear for years, and my husband was confused. Positive change finally began when I forgave my parents. My husband and children didn't know why, but all of a sudden I didn't get mad, scream, throw things, or look at them with hate in my eyes. All of that had become normal for them, but no longer.
>
> I'm so grateful God worked in my life while the children still lived at home. God used the last few years before they graduated from high school to allow them to see a healthy mom. Today, I have wonderful, warm relationships with my grown kids. It's a miracle of God's grace. God deserves all the honor and glory for His ability to restore our broken relationships.

What do you think Beth's children learned about forgiveness early in their lives? Nothing, except that it seemed impossible. What do you think they learned about it when Beth modeled it in the most painful relationships of her life? Plenty! One of the lessons we learn from Beth is that it's never too late to learn to forgive.

Like us, our children live with the bumps and bruises of life, and sometimes with devastating wounds. One of the greatest privileges of being a parent is to help our kids tap into the vast, deep, wide forgiveness of God so they can forgive those who hurt them. They probably won't be able to do that unless we're drinking from that tap first.

• • •

From all we've seen in this book, we realize parenting is as much art as science. In fact, it's much more about building trust and imparting love than controlling a child's behavior. It's our solemn responsibility and our great privilege to pour grace and truth into our kids. As we take the initiative to address these important topics (and many others that inevitably arise), we won't have all the answers. It's perfectly fine to say, "I don't know," yet we can follow that statement with, "but let's find out." We may not be experts, but we can be lifelong learners.

At every point in raising your children—whether they're toddlers asking their first questions or teenagers who question everything—ask God for wisdom, talk to other parents you respect, read to acquire the insights of professionals, and keep the dialogue with your kids open, honest, and positive. "Dialogue" implies that we listen. We may not agree, and in fact, our kids' perspectives may sometimes confuse and outrage us, but we still need to listen. If we listen to them, they just might listen to us.

Our goal as parents isn't merely to make our children conform to our standards, but to point them to God's kindness, truth, grace, and righteousness. We trust Him to do what only He can do: give our children a heart to love and follow Him for the rest of their lives.

Endnotes

1   Diane Levin, PhD, cited in "Talking with Kids About News,"
www.pbs.org/parents/talkingwithkids/news/talking_1.html

2   For example, see "Gestures, Body Language, and
Nonverbal Behavior: Selected References," cited at
www.tirfonline.org/wp-content/uploads/2014/01/
GesturesBodyLanguageNonverbalBehavior_
SelectedReferences_10December2013.docx

3   Elizabeth Gaskell, *North and South* (London: Penguin
Books, first published 1855, this edition 1995), 121.

4   "Three out of every eight Sundays," cited in "7 Startling
Facts: An Up Close Look at Church Attendance in America,"
Kelly Shattuck, Church Leaders, www.churchleaders.com/
pastors/pastor-articles/139575-7-startling-facts-an-up-close-
look-at-church-attendance-in-america.html

5   Charles H. Spurgeon, *Spiritual Parenting* (New Kensington,
PA: Whitaker House, updated edition, 2003), 11.

6   Dr. Tim Elmore and John Maxwell, *Nurturing the Leader
within Your Child* (Nashville: Thomas Nelson, 2004), 126.

7   "You Can't Heal What You Can't Feel," Dr. David B.
Hawkins, Crosswalk, October 10, 2011, www.crosswalk.com/
family/marriage/doctor-david/you-can-t-heal-what-you-can-t-
feel.html

8   Cited by Philip Yancey in *Reaching for the Invisible God* (Grand Rapids: Zondervan, 2001), 69.

9   "Suicide Rates Rise Sharply in U.S." Tara Parker-Pope, New York Times, May 2, 2013, www.nytimes.com/2013/05/03/health/suicide-rate-rises-sharply-in-us.html?_r=0

10   These stages were originally defined and described by Elisabeth Kübler-Ross in *On Death and Dying* (New York: Routledge, 1969).

11   "Advertising: How Many Marketing Messages Do We See in a Day?" David Lamoureux, www.fluiddrivemedia.com/advertising/marketing-messages/

12   "The Average Teenager Sends 3339 Texts Per Month [Stats]," Ben Parr, October 14, 2010, mashable.com/2010/10/14/nielsen-texting-stats

13   C. S. Lewis, *Mere Christianity* (New York: HarperCollins, 2001), 122.

14   "Discovering and Developing Your Child's Strengths," Jenifer Fox, www.parentsleague.org/publications/selected_articles/discovering_and_developing_strengths/index.aspx

15   Statistics: datacenter.kidscount.org

16   American Blended Family Association, www.thebonded-family.com/aboutus

17   Cited in "Church Divorce Rate Way Lower Than Anyone Thought," Paul Strand, CBN News, June

19, 2014, www.cbn.com/cbnnews/us/2014/June/
Church-Divorce-Rate-Way-Lower-than-Anyone-Thought/

18 "After divorce: when to tell the kids that mom or dad is
dating," Linda Ranson Jacobs, July 29, 2014, blog.dc4k.org/
archives/2725

19 Cited in "How to tell your child you're getting divorced," by
Ziba Kashef, Baby Center, www.babycenter.com/0_how-to-tell-
your-child-youre-getting-divorced_3657051.bc

20 From a telephone interview with Linda Ranson Jacobs on
November 14, 2014.

21 Michele Borba, "Bad Friends," in *The Big Book of Parenting
Solutions: 101 Answers to Your Everyday Challenged and Wildest
Worries* (New York: Jossey-Bass, 2009), 314–322.

22 The principles in this section are taken from a series of
sermons by Rod Loy called "You've Got a Friend in Me." My
teaching to the children in our church was based on his research
and teaching.

23 Chris Knoester et al., "Parenting Practices and Adolescents'
Friendship Networks," Journal of Marriage and Family, 2006,
68:1247–1260.

24 "Divorce Study: Financial Arguments Early in Relationship
May Predict Divorce," Huffington Post, July 16, 2013, www.
huffingtonpost.com/2013/07/12/divorce-study_n_3587811.
html

25 "Credit Card Debt Statistics," September 23, 2014, www.
nasdaq.com/article/credit-card-debt-statistics-cm393820

26 "Americans owe $1.2 trillion in student loans," New York Daily News, May 17, 2014, m.nydailynews.com/news/national/americans-owe-1-2-trillion-student-loans-article-1.1796606

27 David Foster Wallace, Kenyon College Commencement Address, 2005, www.theguardian.com/books/2008/sep/20/fiction

28 "Credit Card Basics: Everything You Should Know," Luke Landes, Forbes, June 11, 2013, www.forbes.com/sites/moneybuilder/2013/06/11/credit-card-basics-everything-you-should-know/

29 If you wonder if bullying can be categorized as abuse, see nobullying.com/is-bullying-abuse/

30 StopBullying.gov

31 Statistics from NoBullying.com

32 "Bullying perspectives: experiences, attitudes, and recommendations of 9- to 13-year-olds attending health education centers in the United States," Brown SL1, Birch DA, Kancherla V., Journal of School Health, December 2005, pp. 384-392.

33 Cited in "How to Talk to Your Kids about Bullying," Kimberly Horner, Parenting, www.parenting.com/blogs/mom-congress/kimberly-parentingcom/talk-about-bullying

34 Philip Yancey, "An Unnatural Act," Christianity Today, April 8, 1991, 37.

35 Lewis Smedes, Forgive and Forget (New York: Harper & Row, 1984), pp. 79-80.

36   Frederick Buechner, *Wishful Thinking* (San Francisco: HarperSanFrancisco, 1993), p. 2.

37   Lewis Smedes, "Forgiveness: The Power to Change the Past," Christianity Today, January 7, 1983.

38   Tim Keller, *The Reason for God* (New York: Dutton, 2008), 197.

Acknowledgements

Thank you to my parents, Roger Dollar and Elaine Glenn. As a child, you taught me to love God and follow His purposes. I am the man I am today because you instilled the foundation of faith in me from the day I was born. I love you both so much. Thank you for being the best parents I could ever have asked for!

Special thanks to my pastor, mentor, and friend, Pastor Rod Loy. You contributed *so much* to this book! I've learned how to be a great dad by having a front row seat to watch you. Thank you for everything!

Thank you to the leadership and congregation of First Assembly of God in North Little Rock, Arkansas. You give me more opportunities to make a difference than any other kids' pastor I know. Thanks for allowing me to take what I've learned and share it with others.

I want to thank the amazing parents of my High Voltage Kids. Thanks for letting me participate in the spiritual development of your children. I'm committed to doing everything I can to help make you spiritual champions to your kids!

Thanks to my friend, Pat Springle. You helped bring my thoughts and ideas together in a way that would make an impact. I appreciate you so much!

Thank you, Dr. Michelle Anthony, for writing the foreword and shaping my thoughts about parenting. For years I've been a student of your insights about spiritual parenting. I'm honored to have you as part of this book.

About the Author

Brian has been a kids' pastor since 1992. His wife, Cherith, joined him in ministry in 1998. Together they have passionately served children and families in an effort to raise up a generation of lifelong followers of Jesus Christ.

Brian approaches kids' ministry with a cutting-edge style, leading a volunteer staff of over 150 in ministering to the children at First Assembly of God in North Little Rock, Arkansas. Every week, over 600 children gather for high-energy worship, games, and life-changing ministry from their dynamic ministry team.

In 1998, he founded High Voltage Kids Ministry Resources, which creates attention-getting multimedia, Children's Church curriculum, music, and videos. High Voltage Kids Ministry resources have been used in more than 5,000 churches across America. (highvoltage-kids.com)

Brian has a passion for training and equipping other Kids Ministry leaders to be effective in their churches. He has been a featured speaker at many children's pastors' conferences, seminars, camps, and retreats and is the author of *I Blew It.*

Brian's blog is found at www.briandollar.com. He uses the blog to coach other kids' ministry leaders by answering their questions weekly.

Brian and Cherith have a daughter, Ashton, and a son, Jordan. They love spending time together, watching movies, and cheering for the Dallas Cowboys and Dallas Mavericks. They currently reside in Little Rock, Arkansas.

For More Information

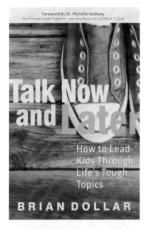

For more information about these and other valuable resources visit **www.salubrisresources.com**

In this book, Brian opens his heart and his life to share his biggest failures as a kid's pastor. Some of the principles are about ministry philosophy, strategy, and communication, but the most important ones—the lessons that will make you laugh and melt your heart—are about the deeper qualities of fear and hope, pride and humility. As you read this book, trust God to change you from the inside out.